International Trade and the Future of the West

John M. Culbertson is Professor of Economics at University of Wisconsin-Madison. He has been an economist with The Board of Governors of the Federal Reserve System, consultant to the Federal Reserve Bank of St. Louis, the Subcommittee on International Finance of the House Banking and Currency Committee, and the USAID Mission to Bolivia. He also toured Southeast Asia for the U. S. Information Agency and lectured on monetary economics at University of Paris. He is the author of four earlier books.

INTERNATIONAL TRADE AND THE FUTURE OF THE WEST

John M. Culbertson

21st Century Press
P.O. Box 5010, Madison, WI 53705

Copyright © 1984 by John M. Culbertson.
All rights reserved.
Printed in the United States of America.

The text of this book was set in 10/12 Garamond
by Landmann Associates, Inc., Madison, Wisconsin

First Edition

Library of Congress Cataloging in Publication Data

Culbertson, John M.
  International trade and the future of the West.

  Includes bibliographical references and index.
  1. Commerce. I. Title.
HF1411.C82   1984   382   84-8699

ISBN 0-918357-00-4 (h. c., trade)
ISBN 0-918357-01-2 (pbk., trade)
ISBN 0-918357-02-0 (pbk., text)

21st Century Press, P. O. Box 5010, Madison, Wis. 53705

to Fran

Contents

	Preface	ix
1	International Trade in Today's World	3
2	Basic Ideas on International Trade	25
3	Effects of International Trade	53
4	The Harmonious-Trade Area and International Trade	99
5	Patterns of International Trade	127
6	Truths and Fictions on International Trade	159
7	Constructive Policies on International Trade	201
	Notes	227
	Index	237

Preface

This book discusses for the general reader, as well as for economists and students of economics, the threat posed by international trade to the United States, to the West, and to all of the world. This is a critically important practical problem for the years ahead. The success or failure with which it is handled will affect all aspects of human life.

The subject must be approached in terms of the free-trade doctrine of the orthodox economics, on which the trade policies of the West recently have been based. Economics textbooks have depicted "free trade" as being mutually beneficial to the nations involved. As is shown here, free trade actually is economically leveling, and is generally damaging to high-income nations. Once it is clear that the traditional "free trade" *or* "protectionism" is a misleading framework for interpreting this subject—"mutually beneficial trade" *or* "economically leveling trade" being more to the point—it is obvious that the whole subject has to be reformulated. An effort was made here to treat the subject in a way that would be useful to a variety of readers. I believe the reader who has not studied economics can make sense of the argument—though he or she may have to skip over a few allusions and references—and that students of economics at all levels will find the ideas accessible.

At the other extreme of readers, I think economists will find the essential points clearly enough stated and the essential references made. The details of the elaborate structure of the economic theory of international trade do not merit discussion here. Their conclusions are built into their assumptions and conventions. The identification of the errors in their foundations leaves the structures without interest.

Economists are not above criticism for jumping from theoretical abstractions to policy recommendations—such as the "liberal" trade policies that are characterized here as threatening to drag the world economically downward. As the potential authors of such a catastrophe, economists perhaps might feel moved to a bit more open mindedness, more concern for realities, less preoccupation with group dogmas than have been the recent norm. I hope that economists will resist the natural inclination to reject out of hand this challenge to their traditional doctrines, and will make reading this book the occasion for a basic rethinking of the subject, of the taken-for-granted assumptions on which the conclusions of orthodox economic theory depend, and of the proper relation of economics to present-day empirical science and its view of the world.

It will be clear that the reinterpretation of economics that is here applied to the subject of international trade is not limited to this subject. The approach will be applied in other subject areas, working toward the formation of a comprehensive, realistic economics.

I am indebted to Frances Culbertson, Amy Culbertson, and Rebecca Boudewyns for comments on the manuscript of this book.

INTERNATIONAL TRADE and THE FUTURE OF THE WEST

1

International Trade in Today's World

The shift of jobs and major industries in recent years from high-wage Western nations to low-wage nations will be ruinous to the West if it continues. The meaning of this shift is not understood in the United States, because it is interpreted in terms of an "economic theory" that is unrealistic. This theory says that "free trade"—or profit-seeking dealings across national boundaries by firms and individuals—automatically will work out for the best for each nation. But experience does not accord with this theory. Japan and other nations that have achieved great economic success in recent years (the counterpart of failures of the United States and the West) do not accept this theory. Their policies have been based on a quite different interpretation of how international trade works, and what its effects are.

The interests of the United States and the West, and in the long run the interests of all nations, require basing the economic policies of nations on realistic analysis of the effects of international trade, rather than on misleading economic theories. Only on the basis of such analysis can international trade be handled in a way that actually will benefit each of the nations involved, and will be the ruination of no nation.

Underlying the issue of how to think about international trade is the larger question of how the world really works. Is this a world that is governed by verbal "principles"—so that the way to success is to follow "principles" that are revealed by making assumptions and theorizing on the basis of them? Or are these "principles" mere delusions? Are the events of the world determined by material causes, rather than verbal "principles"? Is this a cause-and-effect world, as the modern sciences say it is?

If world events reflect the words and stories that are called "principles," then perhaps it is conceivable that success is to be sought through "free trade," or "competition and the free market"—or, some say, through "socialism and public ownership of the means of production." But if this is a cause-and-effect world, none of these verbal formulas provide a valid basis for estimating the actual outcomes of various sets of causal factors and circumstances. Nations that base their policies on the view that this is a cause-and-effect world recently have done much better than those basing their policies on the prevailing kind of economic theory. Earlier history, and earlier dramatic episodes of the economic rise and decline of nations, tell the same story.

To interpret the effects of international trade in terms of cause-and-effect analysis would be to approach it within the thought-world of modern science, within the intellectual framework that has produced so many achievements and successes in other fields in recent decades. The idea of thus interpreting economies in terms of knowledge-based analysis goes far back in history. But Western economics in recent decades has abruptly swung away from this approach, to an orientation toward abstract "economic theory." It has turned from searching for knowledge in experience to searching for what are called principles in mathematical models based on conventional assumptions.

All things considered, the present situation calls for an urgent effort to achieve realistic knowledge and analysis of the workings and the effects of international trade, and to seek this in evidence and experience, that is, to approach the interpretation of economies in the way the successful fields of science approach their subjects. This book represents an effort to take this approach. If the kind of human intellectual and organizational powers that now are available can be effectively applied to this task, it should be possible to devise policies that will make international trade in the troubled world of the late twentieth century a force for human betterment rather than for human disorganization and decline.

International Trade and the Potential Decline of the West

The United States and the Western industrial nations have suffered in recent years an extraordinary loss of the industries and the jobs on which their economic well being had been based. They have been afflicted with persistent deficits in their international payments, which continue. As a result of these great deficits in international payments, the United States is approaching the status of a debtor nation, of being, on net, in debt to foreigners. These factors impose downward pressure on wage rates and living standards.

The other side of the loss of industries and attractive jobs by Western nations is the gaining of these industries and jobs by other countries, mainly by Japan, Taiwan, South Korea, and some other rapidly rising Asian nations. These nations have experienced sharp increases in wage rates and living standards, as well as surpluses in their international trade and international payments.

Such abrupt shifts in the economic positions of nations caused by international trade have played a large role in history. The great rise of Britain to its unique eighteenth-century position of economic eminence and power, for instance, rested on Britain's gaining from other nations the rewarding industries of that time. The other side of Britain's economic rise was the limited advancement or the decline of nations from which it won the rewarding industries: Italy, Spain, Portugal, France. The record of experience offers many illustrations of the power of international trade to drag some nations rapidly downward as it raises others upward.

The recent great loss by the United States and other Western nations of jobs and industries in which high incomes had been earned has undercut the levels of wage rates and standards of living to which Western nations have been accustomed. These nations have not yet made the reductions in wage rates and living standards required to adjust to their reduced economic circumstances, to balance their international payments.

This will not be an easy thing for them to do. The painful need to give up accustomed benefits and newly won advances in living standards can cause political conflicts and irrational government actions, leading to self-feeding processes of national economic decline. The high living standards of the Western nations have been built into fixed costs and a structure of life that cannot quickly be modified. For national economies, even more than for individuals, a rise in living standard is easily accommodated, but adjusting to a decline is onerous, and can be demoralizing.

But the difficulties and costs to Western nations of being economically integrated through international trade with the nations so far involved will be not nearly so great as the difficulties and costs that could result from the extension of this economic integration to nations with enormously greater populations of low-wage labor that have not yet been importantly involved, mainly China and India.

The implications of economic integration through international trade of high-wage Western societies with these high-achieving but low-wage Asian nations have not been realistically interpreted in the United States because of the misleading influence of the currently dominant "theoretical economics" or "economic theory." Economists and policy-makers have taken seriously the doctrine of theoretical economics that unregulated trade across national boundaries cannot damage the interests of nations. They have accepted the claim of economics textbooks that a high-wage nation cannot be damaged by the loss of its industries and jobs resulting from the opening of unregulated trade with a low-wage nation.

The key to understanding what is happening to the West, the fundamental decline in the economic position of the West in recent years, lies in recognizing that this doctrine is erroneous. It is quite inconsistent with experience.

It would not be reasonable to blame the nations that have understood the effects of international trade and have availed themselves of the opportunity to advance themselves rapidly by tapping the markets and taking over the industries and jobs of the vulnerable, high-wage Western nations. The realism with some nations have analyzed the situation, and the skill and efficiency with which they responded to the opportunity it presented to them, are admirable, and provide useful lessons for the future.

But to play out to its bitter end the scenario now being enacted will, in the end, be damaging all around. What is needed is a reconsideration of the rules within which this economic game is being played, and of the theories and ideas that gave rise to those rules. If the effect of international trade is not—as orthodox economic theory claims—to make each nation better off, but is rather to equalize incomes by moving industries and jobs from high-wage to low-wage nations, then international trade could have a devastating effect on high-wage nations. In the long run, its effect could be to impose overpopulation-caused poverty on all of mankind.

To achieve a pattern of international trade that actually will benefit each nation, and will drag no nations downward, then would require a different set of rules and arrangements for international trade. For constructive and realistic thought on this subject, this is the basic question: "What arrangements for international trade *actually, realistically*, will have the effect of bringing benefits to each nation, and damaging or ruining no nation?

It would not be realistic to attribute all of the current economic difficulties of the Western nations to the changing pattern of international trade and international shifts of industries. Many nations would in any case have to suffer the consequences of ill-chosen policies, institutions, and laws, their generation of inflation, of conflicts among economic groups, the blunting of incentives to work and production, the upward push of wages and incomes, great increases in government spending, large government deficits, lax standards of work and workmanship, and ill-considered economic regulations and taxes. Moreover, it can be argued that the terms of trade Western nations enjoyed with other countries when they had a virtual monopoly on production in many industries were unreasonably favorable to the West. For people with much lower wage levels to have to buy their autos, steel, and many other goods at prices that reflected the very high wage rates earned by American workers in those industries was perhaps not a reasonable or sustainable situation.

But the remarkable economic decline of the West cannot be explained by these factors. Even an exemplary economic performance would not have spared the West a great loss of industries and jobs. To understand what is going on, and what lies ahead, requires a realistic interpretation of the implications of the international economic integration that has been proceeding rapidly.

The plight in which the West now finds itself—and the much worse plight that could lie ahead—call for an urgent effort to put aside oversimplified beliefs and develop a realistic understanding of international trade and its implications. Once an accurate understanding of the operating economic processes is achieved, it will be possible to develop arrangements for international trade that actually will do what "free trade" has erroneously been asserted to do, that is, to provide benefits to each nation, while destroying the economic future of no nation.

The New Knowledge and Science: Cause-and-Effect Economics

Informed people now think about processes of change in human institutions and other living systems in a way that has been radically transformed during the centuries since the still-dominant theory of international trade was formulated by Adam Smith. Several revolutions in human thought have occurred since that time. The Darwinian revolution gradually caused earlier notions that the earth was created and designed for human benefit by God or Nature to be replaced by cause-and-effect explanations of events. The discovery of the processes of evolution through "natural selection" by which living systems are formed and continually changed brought about a basic transformation in the way living systems were interpreted. Human beings and their behavior, customs, business firms, nations, and national economies are to be understood within this new framework of knowledge about evolving systems.[1]

The new knowledge made clear that the ideas of earlier times on *how knowledge of the world is to be gained* were fallacious. In the eighteenth century when individualistic economics was formulated, it was widely believed that the ideas we find in our minds were put there by God or Nature. Thinking about the matter in this way, it seemed that if some idea or opinion appealed to us very strongly, that could be taken to show that it had been placed there supernaturally, and must be true.

Thus, economic theory was thought to be properly created by making deductions from "self-evident truths," or "basic principles." Critics of this kind of economics argued that the ways of the world must be learned from evidence and experience, rather than by using our preconceptions as the basis for manipulations of words and equations. Such proponents of an empirical economics and a realistic economics were influential during some periods of time, but in recent years their work has been virtually pushed out of sight.

Another outmoded idea that has been important in shaping the prevailing economic theory is the conception that the world is governed by "laws" or "principles" that are simple and universal. Newton's discovery that the motions of the heavenly bodies could be described by a simple formula was widely misinterpreted as implying that eventually all things would be discovered to be described by simple formulas. It was held that the truth was necessarily simple; the seeming complexity of events was only a smoke-screen, behind which was hidden the truth, which was simple.

Theoretical economics still operates within this kind of framework. Its business is taken to be discovering simple, universal "principles of economics." But as fields of science have built up their knowledge, and have been permitted to look beneath the surface of things with their new instruments, what they have found is a world that became not ever simpler but in many respects ever more complex. The four physical elements of classical thought have been replaced with more than a hundred elements. It turned out that matter is made up of molecules, which are made up of atoms, which are made up of sub-atomic particles.

But the newly understood complexity of nonliving matter is nothing compared to the complexity of of the living things created by evolutionary processes. In Adam Smith's time living things were taken for granted, as miraculous or beyond understanding. Now they are understood to be wonderfully complex, organized, self-maintaining, adaptive systems. But the myth of a world governed by simple, verbal "principles" has continued to dominate some subject fields down through the centuries in which the real world was being shown to be actually of a quite different character.

A difficulty in efforts to create a realistic economics is the continued influence of patterns of thought and language-use that carry over from outmoded conceptions of the way the world works. It is customary in economics to treat words, or imaginary entities that exist only as words, as explaining events. But to say that unregulated international trade is automatically beneficial because of "the principle of comparative advantage," or "competition," or "the free market," "the price system," or "economic theory," is only to play a game of words. Such verbal formulas are offered in place of explanations of events in terms of real actions, the causal processes that actually are operating, the laws and institutions that actually shape actions and events.

To deal with the realities of economies requires forming the habit of pushing aside such purported explanations in terms of a "principle," or "economic law," or "theory," or "model," and looking for the causal factors that actually are determining events. It is necessary to keep in mind that such an asserted "principle" or "theory" may be nothing but an appealing fiction, a modern type of myth, which purports to explain events without making any reference to the actual causal factors.

Another difficulty with the use of language in economics is the hidden meaning or bias of many of the terms that are widely used. Unregulated or individualistic trade across national boundaries commonly is called "free trade." This terminology implies that what is at issue is a choice between "freedom" and "unfreedom" or "tyranny" in trade. But this is not a reasonable view of the matter. An opposite bias could be imparted by replacing "free trade" with "anarchic trade" or "lawless trade." It is desirable to use words that do not have any such hidden meaning or an emotional message, but in economics that requires constant care, and the avoidance of some widely used terms.

In developing an economics that is consistent with present-day scientific thought and knowledge, help recently has become available from the *New Realist* approach to the philosophy of science. In the past, "idealist" philosophy has buttressed an economics oriented to verbal "principles." The recent philosophy of science of "logical positivism" has supported a ritualistic emphasis on procedures in science, and the support of procedures that were not well suited to the social sciences. Thus this philosophy has been taken to justify the preoccupation of recent theoretical economics with certain conventionalized exercises of mathematics and statistics as being what is "scientific."

The New Realist approach directs attention to the structures and processes of the real world, as these have been revealed by the work of the successful sciences. It is helpful in showing the fallacy of a "science" that consists of psychologically satisfying "theories" and mathematical and statistical rituals, and in supporting the need to create concepts and models that relate to the structures and processes actually causing the events in question.[2]

Other important resources have become available for use in developing a modern, cause-and-effect economics, or a *causal economics*. These include the detailed new understanding of evolutionary processes and the structures that govern them,[3] the new comprehension of complex and interactive systems provided by the systems approach,[4] the knowledge provided by cybernetics of the role of error-controlled feedback systems in complex living things,[5] the new capabilities to simulate complex interactive systems that are provided by the availability of computers,[6] the work with similar or analogous kinds of systems being done by biologists and ecologists, and the contribution of economic history and other reality-oriented studies in interpreting the growing body of evidence and experience on how economies work.

Surely, moreover, there is much to be learned from the changes that have occurred in the economic positions of nations since the Second World War, and yet a good deal more to be learned from all of the economic events that have transpired in the two centuries since the ideas on international trade of the orthodox economics were given the form they still retain.

It is anomalous that the theoretical economics that now dominates the beliefs and policies of the United States and most other Western nations still basically recounts Adam Smith's story of the automatic beneficence of unregulated international trade,[7] quite as if the intellectual revolutions and the revolutionary discoveries of the intervening centuries had never occurred. But such is the state of affairs. As Routh says, "The paradigm that provides the inner framework for economic thought has not changed since the seventeenth century."[8] The economic policies of the United States and other nations rest on curious and archaic beliefs from an intellectual world that is long dead. The situation thus calls for a basic rethinking of the subject of international trade, within the framework of present-day scientific thought.

New Circumstances and the New Potential Effects of International Trade

The effects of international trade depend on the circumstances of the times. In using past experience as a guide to the effects of international trade, it must be kept in mind that trade across national boundaries has been radically transformed in recent decades by changes in conditions. Economic integration among the diverse nations of the world now can proceed much further than it could in the past, and can more radically affect all aspects of human life.

Until recently, the potential of international trade for good and for ill could be realized only to a small degree. A number of causal factors acted to prevent trade across national boundaries from working out to its full potential effects. Many of these factors that limited the effects of international trade have been removed, mainly in the past few decades. Thus international trade could now have an effect on the pattern of human economic and social life that is quite different than in the past. Let us briefly review the factors that have brought about this transformation in the effects of international trade.

the revolutionary changes in transportation and communications

In earlier times, much of the international trade that otherwise could have taken place was ruled out by the cost and slowness of transportation and communications. But decade by decade, and with radical jumps in recent decades, technical improvements have reduced this barrier. The steamship, the supertanker, the superfreighter, the airplane, the jet airliner—these have radically cut the cost and the time required for shipping goods and for moving managers and other personnel from one country to another. Technological change has radically shrunken the world. Distance does not have the meaning it used to have.

Similarly, the development of world-wide communications through telephone cables, and then through the use of satellites, means that the factory in Hong Kong or Bombay no longer is out of touch for weeks; it is as close as the telephone. Yet more recently, the development of computers and facilities for virtually instantaneous transmission of large bodies of data implies that paperwork has become a potential element in international trade. The insurance company, for example, can shift its record-keeping functions and the jobs involved from the United States to Taiwan in pursuit of lower wage rates.

Because of these technical developments, the proportion of economic activities and jobs that can feasibly be shifted to a foreign country is now very much greater than in the past.

the end of the colonial status and political disorder that earlier excluded much of the world's population from wage competition with the West

As late as the 1940s, the world's second-largest nation, India, was not available as an open source of cheap-labor competition for the West because it was a British colony, and its economy and international trade were managed by Britain to avoid such competition. Indonesia was a Dutch colony. What now is Vietnam was French Indo-China. Areas that now have a population of well over a billion were thus "managed" so as to supplement rather than compete with Western economic activities. All of that ended after the Second World War, as these areas became independent nations.

The world's most populous nation, China, with its present billion-plus people, suffered from internal turmoil, then civil war, and then the gyrations of Chairman Mao's ideological scripts until recently, and thus has been virtually excluded from providing low-wage labor competitive with Western labor. Its role in the latter 1980s and 1990s is uncertain. It depends on the shifts in power among potential Chinese leaders with different ideas—and thus is governed by no "principle" or "theory."

A pool of low-wage labor involving a population of more than two billion persons, which had been excluded by circumstantial factors, thus could now participate actively in the determination of the level of wage rates and living standards in any group of nations that are economically integrated by international trade.

the erosion of cultural and religious barriers between nations; the spread of world uniculture

In earlier times, the participation of a large part of the world's population in wage labor in Western-style factories was inhibited by local cultures, traditions, and religions. This remains true to a degree in some areas of the world, parts of Africa and the Middle East, for example. But in recent decades, with the shrinking of the world, the spread of television, and its transmission of a secular uniculture through the world, these impediments to world economic integration have been greatly diminished. Perhaps in Asian nations that are the home of a large part of the world's population they have virtually disappeared as an effective impediment to international wage competition.

the development of multinational corporations as anational profit-seekers capable of shifting industries between nations

A factor that in the past was decisive in many cases in preventing low-wage labor in other parts of the world from effectively competing with Western labor was the difficulty of getting the production organized, managed, and financed in the low-wage nation. Local firms and businesspeople were not capable of setting up giant production operations using the latest production methods and management techniques. The local governments could not effectively carry out such operations. Some international firms existed, but they were few, limited in the industries in which they operated, and ordinarily tied to particular Western nations.

Thus it was an event of potentially revolutionary implications when in recent decades there developed giant multinational corporations capable of shifting large-scale production operations from one country to another, applying the latest engineering and managerial techniques, providing capital and skilled managers on whatever scale was needed, adapting to the local conditions in various nations, and utilizing efficient ties to the markets of the Western nations.

Moreover, these corporations largely lost their *national* character. They became anational, acultural instruments for making money, for maximizing the rate of return on the dollars invested, without any lingering emotional concern for the future of England, for the welfare of the United States, for the state of human civilization, or for anything else.

the changed role of political and ideological impediments to international trade

In some earlier times, it seemed that the political and ideological barriers excluding large bodies of potential low-wage labor from competition with the West were fixed, durable, certain to continue at least for some decades. The ways of the King of Siam and of the Stalinist Soviet Union seemed reliably predictable. In recent times, the political arrangements and ideologies that have excluded great bodies of people from integration into world wage competition are more uncertain, unpredictable. The outcome of an election, or the shift in status between competing political factions, could bring a change of great world-wide consequences.

Though Japan, Taiwan, South Korea, Hong Kong, and Singapore have been made potent actors in the world economy by their governments, giant India has been largely insulated from the West by the policies of its Socialist government and China by its shifting versions of the Marxist or communist economy. But in both of these cases, future political and ideological developments cannot be predicted with any confidence. A nation does not have to give up its attachment to what it calls socialism to shift to policies that would make its labor force a potent influence on the level of wages in the economically integrated nations of the world. It thus cannot be assumed that workers competing with one another through the influence of trade across national boundaries will not be competing also with across national boundaries will not be competing also with these populations of two billion people—people of demonstrated skill and energy, accustomed by centuries of experience to overpopulation and low wage rates.

the population explosion and the potential world supply of low-wage labor

While radical improvements in transportation and communications were greatly increasing the potential competition with high-wage Western labor of low-wage labor in other parts of the world, the population explosion was increasing the size of this pool of low-wage labor, both in absolute terms and in relation to the population of the West. Because of the relatively stable populations of most Western nations in contrast to the very rapid population-growth in many low-income societies, the West is an island in a growing sea of of low-wage people in overpopulated nations.

The number of people who exist in nations with low wage rates and a basic inability to provide jobs for their people now numbers between two and three billion. China and India provide nearly two billion people. The equalized level of wage rates in an economically integrated world would depend on the relative numbers of people initially in high-wage and low-wage societies. Thus the immense size of the the pool of low-wage labor now potentially available for economic integration with the West is a factor to be kept in mind. If world wage rates were to be equalized through economic integration, those of the West should be expected to be equalized downward by a very large amount.

does the course of events reflect changing circumstances, or does it depend only on "principles"?

The orthodox economics depicts a world governed by "principles," which works in basically the same way irrespective of changes in circumstantial factors. In this, it exemplifies a conception of the world as reflecting an "idea" or an "ideal," as a thing of words rather than of material entities and material causal relations.

Present-day science, of course, takes quite the opposite view. The outcome of evolutionary processes is viewed as dominated by circumstantial factors, and as reflecting no predetermining "principle." We are told that the rise of mammals may have been caused by the accidental factor that a meteorite hit the earth, raising dust clouds that cooled the earth enough to bring extinction to the then-dominant dinosaurs. In cause-and-effect interpretations of the world like those of science, circumstantial factors cut just as much ice as causal factors as do those that dominate our ideologies and popular viewpoints.

This basic methodological issue is very important in interpreting international trade. "Principles" that implicitly reflect the conditions under which international trade was conducted in the 18th century may, it seems, provide a basically false picture of the effects of international trade and international economic integration under the conditions of the late twentieth century.

The Effects of International Economic Integration

What would be the result of applying throughout the world a "principle of freedom of population movement"? The people in low-income and high-unemployment countries would move to the high-income and low-unemployment nations.

What effect would this have? Wage and unemployment rates would tend to equalize throughout the world. The departure of workers from the low-wage nation would raise wage rates there; the absorption of these workers into the high-wage nation would reduce its wage rate. At what level would wage rates and incomes in the various nations be equalized? This would depend on the relative sizes of the high-income population and the low-income population. In the present-day world, the low-income group is much the larger one. Thus the equalized wage rate and standard of living that applied everywhere would be much closer to the one that had applied in the low-income countries. Similarly, the high unemployment and underemployment that characterizes overpopulated societies would be spread throughout all of the nations.

The required decline in wage rates and living standards could cause drastic changes in the high-income countries. People would find their wages and salaries undercut by the new immigrants from low-income countries. To get jobs in the face of this new competition, they finally could have to accept levels of income far below their accustomed ones.

So large a reduction in living standards involves basic changes in the pattern of life: giving up automobiles, shifting the locations of things that had depended on the availability of the auto, adjusting to smaller houses, cheaper foods, changed forms of entertainment, the elimination of costly forms of health care, great cut-backs in education, government programs, and the cost of government. For such fundamental and painful adjustments to be carried through without the rise of political extremism and political disorder is unlikely. When political and social conditions become such that reasonable and realistic government actions are not possible, troubles beyond reckoning can occur.

But this drastic reduction in the living standard of high-income countries would not be the end of the difficulties. It would be only one stage in the process of economic deterioration. As the high-income nations became low-income nations, all the features that depended on a high standard of living for their existence would disappear. There no longer would be a demand for mass-produced automobiles, aircraft, television sets, advanced medical treatment and its elaborate equipment, scientific and technological research, high levels of education.

In this new situation, technically advanced machinery and methods of production are no longer relevant to the society. The kind of society that has been labelled "advanced" or "developed" would disappear. Adapting to the new set of conditions involves a return to "backwardness," for that is the way people live when the standard of living is low. And in this case there would be no foreign market for advanced goods that could provide a basis for retaining advanced technology.

But the most devastating factor is one that has not yet been mentioned. High-income nations achieve their high incomes because they avoid severe overpopulation. They have low birth rates and low rates of population growth, in some cases stable populations. These result from some combination of causal factors, from cultural norms, national customs, relevant laws and government policies. The low-income nations generally have high birth rates and high rates of population growth. Their overpopulation is a major cause—in many cases, *the* basic cause—of their poverty and low living standard.

In the new situation, with population-integration caused by free population movement, people throughout the world will suffer the effects of high birth rates and rapid population growth that are maintained by any societies or groups. The nations now are all in the same boat. They sink or swim together. A society can no longer protect its standard of living by holding down *its own* birth rate. A high birth rate in any group causes overpopulation that ruins the prospects of all of mankind.

Since there is no prospect that peoples with high birth rates and rapid population growth will immediately change their ways, or that all peoples throughout the world will avoid high birth rates, the standard of living of integrated humanity will be pushed downward by further population growth. In this process, peoples with high birth rates and rapid population growth will come to comprise an ever-larger part of the total population. Any peoples that limit their birth rates will shrink in relative importance, and in power and influence. In a world that does not have population-integration, the society that limits its birth rate saves itself from overpopulation and can achieve a high standard of living. In the world that has population-integration, a group that limits its birth rate causes its own disappearance.

The same kinds of effects that result from the economic integration of humanity through the movement of people follow also from their economic integration through international trade. "Free trade" has the same kinds of effects as "free population movement." The same effects that follow from the movement to the United States of workers from Mexico or India follow also from the movement of industries, factories, and jobs from the United States to Mexico or India—with the output then shipped back to be sold in the United States. Thus, the same basic process of world-wide economic deterioration and movement into backwardness that would result from the international movement of populations would result from sufficiently extensive "free trade."

Just as integration by trade into world-wide job competition would deprive the nation of the ability to set its own standards in population limitation, it would deprive it also of the ability to set its own standards in other matters. The nation that tried to set high standards in working conditions or worker protection would find itself undersold by foreign production, find its industries moving abroad where production is cheaper, where worker-protection costs can be avoided. The same is true of standards in environmental protection, resource conservation, aesthetic considerations—standards that reflect any consideration other than the cheapness of production. In production standards as well as in population limitation, world economic integration would enforce a lowest-common-demominator competition. Low standards undercut high standards. Low standards are thus enforced on all.

World economic integration thus deprives the nation, acting through its government, of the powers and capabilities that are needed to guide and protect the economic welfare of its people. Under world economic integration, national governments are thrown into competition with one another to gain industries and jobs for their people. A government placed in this position lacks the ability to regulate business, to protect the nation's future, to guide its destiny in one direction or another.

National governments would lose—are now losing—powers and capabilities that have long been considered essential attributes of nationhood. There is no higher-level organization in the world to take over functions that nations become incapable of performing, or to take the place of the nation as the major organizing unit for human affairs. The result would be a movement toward impotent government, toward a quasi-anarchy for mankind.

It may seem incredible that a policy so widely extolled as unregulated international trade, or "free trade," could have such terrible consequences. But it must be kept in mind that this unregulated trade has been talked about as an "ideal" a "principle," in terms of abstract economic theory. This idealized "free" or unregulated trade has not been widely practiced. The economically successful nations have not achieved their success by following such policies. The world of words within which unregulated trade has been so praised has had little connection with the world of actual economic events, with the record of experience.

It must be kept in mind also that unregulated trade across national boundaries is really a radical policy. Such trade would economically integrate the nations of the world, would integrate peoples, undercutting the powers and the existence of nations. Would anyone propose thus integrating all the firms of the nation into one unit, or all the football teams, or all the religions, or all the cities? On the face of things, such an arrangment would not *work*. It would eliminate the organizational framework within which things get done.

It also is true that such unregulated trade is fundamentally *unnatural*. Not only human beings, but all living species are organized into groups that are to a degree separated or insulated from one another. Animals and plants exist in territorial groupings. Biologists tell us that this is essential to their evolution and their survival. This is the way they avoid "putting all their eggs in one basket," and achieve the variety or diversification that permits them to "experiment," to explore alternative developmental paths, to reduce the hazard that a change in conditions will cause all of the groups to fail, and cause the species to become extinct. Biologists tell us that the loss of variety is the road to extinction. They tell us also that integration and loss of their territorial groupings would undermine the population-control systems of the higher animals (and thus their habitat-preservation arrangements), just as it does for humans.

And, of course, human beings always have operated in territorial groupings, the tribe or band, the clan, the city-state, the principality, the kingdom, the empire, the modern nation. Particular kingdoms or nations rise and decline. Some disappear. The advance of mankind has derived from diversity, from experimentation. Patterns that bring success spread, through conquest or copying. Patterns that bring failure tend to drop out of the picture. The logic of evolution applies as much to human institutions, societies, civilizations as to other living systems.

The familiarity and appeal of its slogans thus do not imply that "free trade" is an experience-tested or a natural condition. It is neither of these. The appeal that comes from immunerable repetitions of the slogans, "free trade," "cooperation," "solidarity," "unity," "elimination of barriers"—this should not blind us to the fact that the policies in question are in basic conflict with the ways of the world.

Constructive Policies for International Trade

The "official" view of international trade in the United States and some other Western nations has been that "free trade"— unregulated and unrestricted trade across national boundaries by individuals and firms—is the best possible arrangement. In the usual way of putting matters, the only alternative to "free trade" is "protectionism," defined as restrictions on international trade serving the interests of particular firms or groups of workers, to the detriment of the nation, and the world.

This obviously is not an accurate characterization of the different kinds of policies toward international trade that are to be considered. The policies of nations that have achieved rapid economic advancement by using international trade, such as Japan in recent years, surely were different from both "free trade" and "protectionism." The implicit argument, "Since 'protectionism' is obviously foolish, you therefore have no choice but to adopt 'free trade' " is a misleading one.

A reasonable approach to the subject must analyze realisically the effects that actually would be caused by different systems of international trade under the conditions that now exist. What actually will happen if people are permitted to move "freely" among nations, if people and firms are "free" to ship goods and transfer services and funds among nations?

A basic question is this: "What kind of policies would be required to cause a situation in which international trade would bring benefits to each nation, and would damage no nation?" The orthodox or individualistic economics asserts that this outcome results from from completely unregulated trade across national boundaries. Unfortunately, this assertion is false, and the widespread faith of Western economists and government officials in this falsehood is the source of much of the mischief and confusion that now afflicts policy toward international trade.

The condition that is asserted, however, is of interest. So a major focus of attention in this work must be the question: "What kind of policies are required *really, actually, truly* to result in international trade that benefits each nation, and damages no nation?" A valid answer to that question plays a central role in the realistic interpretation of international trade.

2

Basic Ideas on International Trade

The ideas on international trade that most people have acquired are quite unrealistic. Those studying economics in the United States have been taught that economic dealings naturally work out for the best, under the guidance of what are really imaginary entities, "the free market," and "competition." But they do not learn, of course, just how this occurs, or how such a thing can happen in a cause-and-effect world. In some other countries, people learn to believe that "socialist planning" is the answer, or Marxism, or The Revolution, or the "rich nations helping the poor nations." These formulas do not deal with actual events and their causes, or relate to the way the world actually works.

As an aid to thinking about international trade in a realistic and scientific way, this chapter sketches a modern interpretation of how the world works—as a replacement for the 18th-century ideas of "natural harmony under individualism" that form the basis of theoretical economics. It also offers twelve theses on international trade that will serve to present basic issues underlying controversies over policy toward international trade.

How Does the World Work—What Is "Natural"?

Modern scientific thought views living things as complex systems, which reproduce themselves with variation, and undergo evolutionary change. Families, religious groups, firms, and nations are living systems of human beings. Species and living systems continually change, in part because of the operation of "selection." Some of them suit the circumstances in which they exist, and thus thrive. They expand or are copied. Others perform badly, or are not suited to the situation that exists. They shift to a new pattern, decline in importance, or are extinguished.

This process of *selection*, or differential growth or shrinkage, survival or nonsurvival, can be thought of as involving "competition." But such competition does not automatically work for human benefit. A moment's thought will bring to mind cases in human affairs in which the low outcompetes the high, the evil outcompetes the good. The mafia outcompetes the legitimate business; exaggerated advertising claims outcompete the truth; the business that disposes of its wastes cheaply and illegally outcompetes the one that pays the price of safe waste disposal. If processes of change in the world are to operate for human benefit, something more than "competition" must guide them.

Indeed, much of the work of governments and other social institutions consists of providing the needed guidance to behavior, discouraging actions and competition of kinds that degrade human beings, and encouraging competition of kinds that works to their benefit. Anarchy, or "anything goes," or "free competition," has been tried many times. It does not work.

Thus, it is not true that what is "natural" is necessarily desirable from a human point of view. That mythical entity, Nature, does not guide events for human benefit. What exists, or is natural, is a cause-and-effect world, in which human beings must cause their own successes, and achieve their own patterns of civilized life.

societal change as a cause-and-effect process

Ongoing evolutionary change in human societies and in other living systems, in the modern scientific view, is strictly a cause-and-effect process. It has no built-in goal. It has no predetermined happy ending. The direction taken by events is determined by the set of causal factors operating in each case. Being governed by its causes, the process of change under natural selection cannot possibly be preprogrammed to offer human beings a gift of automatic "progress," or "economic growth."

A species that survives does so by *causing* its own survival, by behaving in a way that leads to survival in a cause-and-effect world, in the circumstances that actually exist.[1] To cause one's own survival involves meeting many requirements. The local group of the species, such as the colony of bees or the pack of wolves, must occupy its territory so that other species do not invade it, must develop defense mechanisms against parasites and predators, must prevent overpopulation and overfeeding that would destroy its habitat, must avoid intra-group conflict or disorganization that would damage its performance, and so on. Behaviors of animals that in the past were thought of as quaint, or bizarre, have come to be understood as belonging to strategies for meeting the requirements of survival, strategies that are much more complex than was imagined.

As is true of other living systems, a high-income nation must meet a set of requirements if it is to cause its own survival—survival, that is, as a nation with a particular pattern of life and a high standard of living. Societies that achieve this over a period of time do so through accomplishments that often are taken for granted, so their importance is not understood. These include controlling population, protecting the land and resources, maintaining order and harmony so that effective government and production organizations can be achieved. One could make a list of societies that have failed, or that are failing, for want of one or another of these accomplishments.

Such accomplishments of societies arise from their cultures, institutions, laws, and political systems. Nations differ widely in these aspects of their behavior, and in their accomplishments and their failings. The successes and the failures—and the disappearances—of societies, like those of other living systems, reflect their performances, are *caused* by their behaviors.

To continue to survive in a competitive economy, a restaurant must create edible food, a professional basketball team must win some games, an automobile firm must produce cars that run well. Each of these accomplishments is difficult. Many firms fail to meet them, and go out of existence. The required outcomes can be created only by organizations that function well, that use human abilities in a constructive way.

Similarly, the species, the local tribe or band, and the nation must *cause* its own success and survival by generating the required performance. It can generate a behavior that meets the survival-requirements of the external world only by also using its powers and abilities in a way that meets the demands of its environment.[2]

A national society requires organization at a number of levels. All living things consist of multi-level systems. The cell is a very complex system. The organ is a higher-level system made up of cells. The nervous system is yet more comprehensive, and there are the cybernetic regulatory systems that maintain the body's internal temperature, its blood-sugar level, and other conditions required for its survival. At a still higher level is the whole body as an integrated, functional system. The body's many subsystems achieve wonders of adaptive behavior. They nourish the body, regulate its temperature and other internal variables, repel or destroy invading microorganisms, develop resistance to poisons. These functions illustrate the complexity of achievement required for living things to earn survival in the cause-and-effect world.

group behavior; the "social" element in survival-related accomplishments

Human beings and many other species are not adapted to live as isolated individuals. It was not under such a pattern of behavior that they evolved. On the contrary, the person must live and function as a member of organized groups. The interacting behavior of individuals in these structured groups is what achieves the performance required for survival. It is the local group, as a group, that must somehow cause its individuals to avoid destructive internal conflict, and collaborate in holding the territory against invaders. The group or society must cause its individuals to behave in ways that avoid damaging the habitat and the food supply. Otherwise the actions of individuals will cause the failure of the group, and thus of the individuals who can exist only in such a group. To do this, the group or society must bring about behavior by individuals that avoids an overpopulation that would ruin the land and the food supply.

This social or group element in survival-related accomplishments is often ignored or denied. It does not fit in well with political viewpoints and concepts based on the freedom of the individual to do as he or she wishes, or with the idea that Nature guides events to a desirable outcome so long as individuals are free to take whatever actions they like. Thus, even the scientific literature includes inconsistencies on this point. "Freedom" and the granting of individual "rights" often are presented as the answer to political and economic problems— even though it is obvious that producing tractors, steak dinners, or symphony concerts requires people each to meet exactly the requirements of his or her particular assignment—which is the opposite of "freedom" to do as one wishes. And evolution is sometimes interpreted as involving competition only among individuals (or even among "genes"), even though it is obvious, when the point is raised, that individual people survive and live as they do only as members of social groups or organizations, firms, religions, nations.

To continue to survive in a changing world, the species, and the firm, and the nation may have to change and evolve in a direction that is dictated by the changes in its environment. In most cases, survival is not earned by just continuing to behave in an unchanging way. Given that humans and other living things exist in multi-level organizations, this evolutionary change must occur at many different levels. For example, the behaviors of people must change in a way that permits the firms to continue to work well so that the nation can continue to produce effectively and survive in a world that is changing in many ways. Success requires that the pieces of this elaborate, evolving system fit together functionally. Recent great leaps in knowledge about evolutionary structures and processes have made them seem ever more complex and ever more wonderfully organized—even though they do not automatically work to human purposes, and they generate failures and exterminations as well as successes.

effective groups and systems require separateness from outsiders

To maintain their functional organization and ability to perform effectively, so as to meet the external world's requirements for survival, living things necessarily draw a sharp line between themselves and outsiders. The individual body has elaborate defenses against invaders, sharply distinguishing between itself and the outside world—as is illustrated by its rejection of transplanted organs.

The hive of bees has its soldiers at the entrance to destroy invaders. Territorial groups of the higher animals also defend the integrity and effectiveness of the group against invaders, including interloping members of the same species.

Species and subspecies use mating rituals to avoid mating with other species, which would destroy the coherence, the "self-control," and the survival-effectiveness of the species. The tribal man and village man of earlier times similarly resisted the absorption of outsiders, and this was functional, essential to the preservation of the coherence and survival-capabilities of the group.

In the present-day human world, effective organizations similarly draw a sharp line between insiders and outsiders to preserve the integrity and effectiveness of the organization. The Ford Motor Company makes a distinction between people who are members of the firm, and subject to its rules and procedures, and the outsiders who are not. The organization determines who is to be admitted, and who is permitted to retain membership. A military organization draws a sharp line between members and nonmembers. These organizations would be meaningless and ineffective if they did not do so. They would not be *organizations* or *systems* if they did not thus maintain a distinction between what belongs to the organization or system and what does not.

Basic Ideas on International Trade 31

An understanding of the way the world of living things works and the way evolutionary processes operate thus shows the necessity for living things to preserve their organizaitonal units, to insulate themselves from others, to repel invaders, parasites. They must behave in different ways toward insiders who belong to their organization and to outsiders who belong to other organizations.

The universal rule in the world of living things thus is not general integration or all-oneness. It is quite the opposite. It is preservation of the separateness of functional groups and organizations, which is required for their effectiveness, which is required for the performance and the survival of living things.

A business firm such as IBM has relations of different types with many other organizations, with suppliers, consultants, customers, government agencies. In each case, these are arranged by people acting on behalf of the agencies involved. The people involved, thus, are playing roles defined by their organizations, acting on behalf of the organizations. Such structured, functional relationships are what is required to make the world's wheels turn. What would happen if all of the people involved suddenly acted as if they had no obligations to organizations and simply did as they personally wished? The organizations would be meaningless, and the result would be chaos.

The major, the top-level, organization of human beings now is the national society, the nation. It is understandable that the nations that succeed and can continue in their successful pattern of behavior will be those that protect their separateness sufficiently to be able to develop a coherent survival-strategy and effectively pursue it. It is understandable also that they will not be able to do this while permitting their members to take whatever action they wish.

the contrast between natural-harmony individualism and other views of man and the world

This view of how the world works, or what is "natural," of present-day science is not basically inconsistent with most earlier thought on the matter, but in the seventeenth century a doctrine arose that is fundamentally in conflict with both earlier ideas and modern science. This is the conception of the world as having been created by Nature for the purpose of serving mankind. Nature was supposed to have designed the world so that things worked out for the best for mankind when each person did as he or she wished. Opposing all earlier thought and observation on the social character of mankind and the social, moral, and religious structures that underlay the successful human society, this new view made the "freedom" of the individual the answer to virtually all of human problems.

In its more carefully worked out forms, as in the economics of Adam Smith, this doctrine offered an explanation of how humans could be "free" to do as they wished. The explanation was that Nature had, in effect, preprogrammed people so they would behave in the way that was required to make things work out for the best. Man's role was glowingly depicted in natural-harmony ideology as one of "freedom." But the thoughtful person must see that this is the "freedom" of a robot. Man, in this ideology, is Nature's preprogrammed robot.

In this view, organization, design, system, functional effectiveness in human affairs came not from man's intelligence, foresight, knowledge, social systems, moral virtues, or any kind of human achievement—nor, of course, from the trial and error of natural selection. It was all Nature's doing. Man was, like other creatures, only a player acting out Nature's script.

The aspect of this story that gave it great appeal to people was the homeocentric implication that Nature had planned and prepared a virtual heaven on earth—an earthly Garden of Eden—for mankind. In order to claim the wonderful gifts planned for the species by Nature, mankind need not create Eden, or earn Eden, or deserve Eden. Mankind only had to . . . Here the creator of a particular version of the natural-harmony myth would fill in his notion of man's *abracadabra*, the magical key to Nature's promised land.

The version of the myth that was, and has remained, dominant in orthodox economics claims that the key to gaining the fruits of Nature's Plan is individualism. Each person, and business, should be "free" to do as it wishes, should enjoy, in Adam Smith's term, "natural liberty."

Other writers turned the formula in other directions. Marx said the key was The Revolution and the transition to ideal communism. Some said it was public ownership of the means of production, and socialism.

These doctrines all were formulated within the myth of man-serving Nature. They were not based on experience, or on a cause-and-effect interpretation of how the successful society is achieved. Thus, beliefs on this subject came to be dominated by concepts that related not to the world as it actually is, but to the idea that everything automatically worked out for the best when each person did as he or she wished—because Nature, a magical or supernatural Nature, had designed the world to that effect.

The individualistic version of this story implied that the national government should not attempt to plan and manage the affairs of the nation in an effort to achieve its success and survival. That would violate Nature's Plan. And it would intrude into the "rights" that Nature had conferred on people to do as they wish.

The same was true of society, religion, moral leaders. They were not to intrude into the "freedom" that Nature had decreed for people. In thinking that socially responsible behavior and high moral standards were the basis of the effective and civilized society—the natural-harmony ideology said—the earlier thinkers had been wrong. The answer was *each person for himself*. This doctrine constituted a sharp break with virtually all serious human thought of earlier times, and it is no less inconsistent with present-day scientific thought.

cosmopolitanism or one-worldism as derived from natural-harmony individualism

The conception of Nature-ordained individualism gave seeming justification to a one-world or cosmopolitan view of human activities. Given that the nation was not the source of needed organization and guidance but only a potential intruder into the "freedom" of people and businesses, the less the nation did, the better. *Laissez faire* was the answer. Let it be. Leave it to Nature, and to competition. With the nation thus out of the picture as a planner and organizer of human activities, what remained were only the "free" individuals and businesses, operating presumably under the guidance of Nature's Plan.

Removing from the picture all top-level organizers, guides, planners of human activities—roles that had been played by kings, statesmen, theologians and churches, and democratic assemblies—leads to cosmopolitanism, internationalism, a world of free, leaderless, individuals and firms. Removing the nations into which people had been organized leads to worldwide economic integration, with individuals and firms acting in their own interests on a world-wide basis. In a certain view of the world, this is what is natural. It is what is consistent with Nature's Plan.[3]

This view came to be reflected in a set of attitudes and emotionally loaded terms by which the person who opposed individualism and "free trade" was depicted as bigoted, ignorant, or governed by some selfish personal motive. Adam Smith set the subject into this format two hundred years ago. The recent extolling of "free trade" as good, and "protectionism" as backward, selfish, and evil reflects the same viewpoint and vocabulary.[4]

The question to be raised in a realistic treatment of international trade is, "How does the world actually work?" If it is true that Nature has preprogrammed people and the world so that an earthly Eden will arise, under Nature's Plan, if government, society, and morals are kept out of the picture and each person and business does as it wishes—then presumably mankind has little choice but to follow this formula. Who could fight against this miracle-working Nature?

But if this is all a wishful story, which has won such wide support because it promises something for nothing and gives people and businesses a justification for doing what they want to do, then the situation is rather different. In terms of cause-and-effect thinking and the lessons of experience, "each person and each firm for itself" seems to be a formula for societal failure. History provides many illustrations of such failures.

the decisive issue: how does the world work?

So the essential issue in interpreting international trade is whether this is a cause-and-effect world, or a world that works in the manner depicted by Adam Smithian natural-harmony individualism. The choice of the basic intellectual framework within which international trade is to be interpreted is decisive. Logically, Nature-planned individualism says, "Leave it to the self-serving actions of people and businesses. Keep government out of the picture. Deemphasize, or even abolish, the nation. Rely on Nature."

On the other hand, as viewed in terms of modern scientific thought, the belief that if each person does as he or she wishes "Nature" will make things turn out right falls into the realm of myths or superstitions. There is no way in which this conception of the world can be reconciled with present-day knowledge of how the world works. There is no conceivable way in which the required events could actually be caused.

Thus a nation that applies modern knowledge and thought to the problem of achieving and protecting a high standard of living will look toward effective organizations, the intelligent development and application of knowledge, the making of strategic choices on the basis of realistic interpretation of the existing circumstances, the development of a social framework within which people minimize conflict and generate the prerequisites of a high-income, civilized society. The historical episodes of national economic success and failure seem to support this interpretation.

The recent literature and textbooks of economics have supported the free-trade doctrine. They remain implicitly based on the economics of Nature's Plan as developed by Adam Smith—though most economists are not mindful of the origins and foundations of the doctrine. "Modern economic theory" provides only new modes of presenting the doctrine; no new reasons for believing that it describes the realities of the world. The economists and schools of economics that made important contributions to the realistic interpretation of international trade, and the issues they raised, have been ignored in recent economics. Thus there now is a lack of a coherent interpretation of international trade and its implications in terms of the concepts and knowledge of present-day science. To contribute to the understanding of international trade within a realist or scientific economics is a function of this book.

It is important in considering the many issues and controversies relating to international trade to keep in mind that the fundamental and in many cases decisive question is the basic one: "Is international trade to be interpreted in relation to a cause-and-effect world, or in terms of the conception that when each person and firm does as it wishes, Nature's Plan or Nature-designed harmony makes things turn out for the best?"

Basic Issues and Questions: Twelve Theses on International Trade and International Economic Integration

A number of basic issues and points of confusion are posed by the following twelve theses or propositions on international trade. The points discussed here are important for consideration of policies toward international trade.

the effects of a pattern of international trade depend on the set of causal factors operating in each case—not on any "principle"

Practical consideration of cases of international trade and of policy toward international trade always will turn on the issue: "How does the world work? Do events reflect verbal laws or so-called principles, or are they the result of causes?"

Those who have absorbed the orthodox economics will, unless they think about what they are doing, approach any practical problem by trying to fit it into some conventional "principle," or "law," or "model." Thus, it is necessary to keep continually in mind that in modern thought events must be explained only in terms of causes.

In any case of international trade and policies toward international trade, the operating causes are numerous, and they interact in ways that require analysis. The particular circumstances impinging on a nation are often among the most important causal factors at work. The way a set of arrangements for international trade works out in a particular case depends, for example, on transportation costs and the limitations on trade and economic integration they impose, on the relative sizes of the nations involved, on the relation between their wage rates and living standards, on the capabilities of their governments. Any interpretation of international trade that omits such causal factors cannot provide an accurate guide to the way events will work out and the effects of different policies for international trade.

only under special conditions does international trade benefit the nations involved

If Jones and Smith voluntarily arrange a trade or economic deal between themselves, must this not be beneficial to both of them? If it were not, why would they both agree to the deal?

Jones and Smith must both *expect to benefit* from the deal if they voluntarily agree to it, but in such matters what people expect is not necessarily what actually happens. Moreover, one party to the deal may mislead the other one. In cases in which Jones is ill informed or incompetent and Smith is wily and manipulative, the most common outcome will be that Smith will benefit from the deal but Jones will lose.

Another important kind of case is that in which Jones and Smith arrange a deal from which they both benefit, but their benefits reflect the fact that they are taking advantage of McGregor—or that they are collaborating to rob XYZ Company. In nearly all cases, economic deals affect people other than those who make the deals. Thus, the fact that the people who arrange a deal benefit from it does not demonstrate that the deal is desirable or socially constructive. Indeed, a large part of law, custom, and the moral code is oriented to preventing people from taking actions that would benefit themselves at the expense of other people—a point that raises obvious difficulties for the notion of natural harmony under individualism.

No automatic arrangement has been devised that can permit only desirable deals, while precluding undesirable or antisocial ones. A reason for this is that which deals are desirable, and which ones are not, must be a matter of interpretation and judgment, requiring action on behalf of society, in many cases by the national government.

Thus, the general idea that "free" or unregulated economic actions are inherently or automatically beneficial is false. Such deals can be damaging to third parties, and even to one or both of the participants, when all of the actual effects are taken into account. To permit constructive economic actions while preventing destructive economic actions must be accomplished by laws, institutions, and regulations devised by human societies.[5] Successful societies accomplish this; an important source of the failure of other societies is that they do not. The point applies with special force to international economic dealings, for these offer a special kind of opportunity for individuals and firms to take actions that benefit themselves but damage a society.

international trade under "free trade" is not trade between the nations but trade across national boundaries by private parties

The idea that international trade between, say, the United States and Taiwan must benefit both nations, or else it would not occur, reflects confused thinking. Ordinary trade is not arranged between, say, "the United States" and "Taiwan," that is, between the governments of the two nations. If that were the case, it *could* be asserted that the trade must benefit both nations, at least "benefit" them in the opinions of the representatives of the nations who approved the trade deal.

But ordinary "international trade" is not "trade negotiated between nations" but "trade that crosses national boundaries." Such trade is arranged by private parties and firms, acting only in their own private interests. They do not address the question whether their actions are or are not beneficial to the nation. Ordinarily, they would not be in a position to give a valid answer to the question if they did raise it.

Unregulated trade across national boundaries, or ordinary "international trade," thus, occurs only where the private parties involved expect to profit from the deals. But this provides no basis for asserting that the trade is beneficial to both *nations*, or to either nation. In trade across national boundaries, as in other matters, deals that provide profit to those that make them may damage other people, and may damage the public interest, or the nation as a whole.

Basic Ideas on International Trade 39

the logic of the system calls for international trade to be arranged between national governments

The basic logic of the decentralized or "free enterprise" economy is that each person and organization acts on behalf of its own interests—within a framework of laws and rules that limits actions that benefit the actor but damage others and the society. Thus, individuals make deals on their own behalf, taking jobs, signing contracts, investing funds and borrowing money.

Similarly, organizations within the national economy act on their own behalf. To do this, the organization must designate a person or group as its agent, to act on behalf of the organization. It is understood that, say, a purchasing agent for Xerox Corporation is acting on behalf of the Corporation, not acting to make money for his own pocket. For the purchasing agent to seek his own profit, by taking a bribe to give Xerox's business to Firm Z, would be violating the trust imposed in him, violating the rules of the Xerox Corporation, and likely breaking a state law as well. It would seem nonsensical to propose that any employee of Xerox—or even that anyone whatever—should be permitted to take actions affecting the interests of the Corporation, for example, to make a decision as to what it should buy, and from whom, at what price. The organization can be effective, and survive, only if it has control over actions that affect its interests.

The nation is the highest level economic organization of the modern world. The economic success or failure of people and firms is governed largely by the success or failure of the nation to which they belong. Extending the logic sketched above, it is to be expected that *the nation* must act on matters importantly affecting its interests. Like the firm, it will appoint agents or officers who are understood to act on behalf of the nation, not in their own private interests. This is the way the nation operates in making treaties with other nations, and in conducting affairs with them through the government's State Department or Department of Foreign Affairs. The nation develops laws regulating who may enter the nation and controlling relations between its citizens and foreign governments.

Following out this logic, it would be expected that the nation would arrange with other nations the kinds of goods that flow across its boundaries. The flow of these goods affects what industries and what kinds of jobs are located in each nation. A question at issue is: "What industries shall exist in our nation, providing jobs and earning opportunities for our people. And what industries, on the other hand, shall be located in other nations, with us meeting our needs by buying from them?"

For economic dealings across the nation's borders to be conducted by private parties acting for their own profit, and for the industries that are located within the nation to be determined as a side-effect of these self-seeking private actions, seems an anomalous arrangement. It is like letting anyone who wants to do so buy or sell on behalf of Xerox Corporation.

the only way to assure that international trade benefits the nations involved is for it to be arranged between governments

The logic of a self-responsible system of organizing society calls for the interests of Jack Jones to be advanced by the forward-looking actions of Jones, the interests of the Scott Family to be advanced by the planning and actions of members of the family acting on its behalf (rather than for their individual profit), the interests of IBM to be advanced by the planning and actions of members of IBM acting on behalf of the organization, and the interests of the United States to be advanced by planning and actions taken on behalf of the nation, taken by its government.

At each organizational level, there are questions as to what outcome would be "desirable," or what goals and values are to be implemented. There also is a problem of providing the knowledge, wisdom, judgment, and analysis to estimate what actions will, in the prevailing circumstances, be needed to cause the desired outcome. No automatic mechanism, no ritual, will bring about the "right" outcome, magically avoiding the problem of defining what outcome is "right" and what actions actually will cause this outcome.

It is, however, a common pattern of human behavior to bypass the requirements of realistic foresight and retreat into some myth that prescribes formulas or rituals that work as if by magic. The orthodox economics since Adam Smith has argued that for international trade there *is* a ritual that automatically produces the best-possible solution. This is said to be "free trade," or unregulated trade across national boundaries by anyone, by firms and people acting in their own interests.

But except on the basis of preplanning of the world by a magical Nature, such a thing cannot be true. Within a cause-and-effect world, the inputs of chosen goals, of knowledge, of analysis that are required to shape a pattern of international trade that serves the interests of the nation must be provided by agents acting on behalf of the nation, by its government.

unregulated international trade causes economic integration that undercuts the functional organization of human life

Present-day knowledge of living systems shows their dependence on structured organizations at many levels. Each of these organizations must preserve its coherence and separateness. Otherwise it ceases to be an organization, a functional structure.

Human life always has been organized into separate organizations, tribes, city-states, empires, nations. The nation is the highest level organization, and the most important organization, in the existing system of human life. To undermine the coherence and effectiveness of the nation would bring disorder and deprive human affairs of intelligent guidance, would make the human situation an evolutionary anomaly and threaten the collapse of the prevailing pattern of human life—imperfect as that is.

Thus the conception of "one world," or of universal all-oneness or integration of human beings, is not consistent with the realities of the world. Following policies based on this conception could dissolve the organizational structure that is essential to civilized human life.

international economic integration would spread overpopulation-caused poverty throughout the world

Throughout recorded history, human societies have shown a tendency to generate an overpopulation that causes a low standard of living and a shortage of jobs. Some nations, through a combination of circumstances and their cultures and policies, limited or avoided overpopulation-caused poverty. The development of high living standards, and of the technology and knowledge that depended on these, arose from the achievements of these nations. Had universal overpopulation-caused poverty prevailed, the "economic development" of the past two centuries could not have occurred.

The process by which this economic improvement occurred is reversible. The universalization of overpopulation-caused poverty will eliminate the demand for advanced products, the relevance of advanced technology, and the ability to support the system of knowledge, expertise, and specialization on which these depend. A general decline in living standards based on the universal spread of overpopulation-caused poverty will substantially reverse the process by which the advanced nations rose from a narrow, simple, ignorant, and poor life to the conditions that they recently have achieved.

The economic integration of humanity through the free movement of populations or the free movement of goods and services will throw all humanity into the same pot, make humanity one great experiment rather than a set of separate experiments. Within this structure of world-equalized wage rates, the effects of high birth rates in any group or area will be spread to all of the world. And within this structure, high-birth-rate societies will increase in their relative importance by increasing their relative numbers. Within this organizational framework for mankind, for a society to limit its birth rate and its numbers will not have the effect of elevating its standard of living, but only will bring about its decline to a position of relative insignificance and powerlessness.

Because of the potential of a high birth rate and rapid population growth to dominate the economic picture, quite overpowering other factors, the achievement of controlled population always depends on territoriality, or the establishment of separate territorial groups. With this separation, the population-limiting group experiences the benefits of its behavior, prospers, and sets a pattern for others to copy. With population-integration, such example-setting success is impossible. Rapid-population-growth behavior dominates population-limitation behavior and dominates the outcome, which is universal overpopulation, with all of its consequences.

international economic integration would also cause standards-lowering competition of other kinds

In establishing and enforcing a set of rules or social norms within which its people limit the birth rate and avoid overpopulation, the nation is *maintaining a standard* that permits it to have a high level of living and an advanced type of life. The maintaining of such a standard is necessary to bring about the behavior of people that will cause the high level of living. In the absence of such a standard, a degenerative competition will prevail. High-birth-rate behavior and rapid population growth will increase the relative size and importance of a group in society, causing it to dominate the outcome.

The same interpretation applies to other kinds of economic standards. Unless the society defines and enforces standards that prevent this pattern, the firm that disposes of its chemical wastes cheaply by dumping them into the river will undersell its competitors—and thus environment-destroying behavior will be rewarded, will be what is successful, and will become the prevailing practice. Similarly, in the absence of such standards competition will force firms to avoid the costs involved in safeguarding the health and safety of their workers, the costs of conserving natural resources, the costs of protecting aesthetic values.

The natural effect of cost-cutting competition among firms is to drive them to cut costs *by all available means*. No nature-provided mechanism distinguishes socially damaging forms of competition from socially constructive forms, and prevents the former. If competition is to be limited to constructive forms, and socially damaging or ruinous competition is to be avoided, this must be accomplished by societal rules that set the required standards and enforce them. Doing this is one of the functions of the national government.

But unregulated international trade and international economic integration acts to deprive national governments of the ability to maintain such standards. Just as a firm cannot maintain high-standards behavior in the face of competition from low-standards firms, and within the United States a state cannot maintain high standards in the face of standards-cutting competition from other states, a nation cannot maintain high standards in the face of competition from low-standards nations. To do so would cause the loss of industries and jobs to firms operating in low-standards nations. Thus, international economic integration throws nations into a degenerative competition. The nation must reduce or eliminate its production standards to avoid being undercut by other nations and losing the industries and jobs it needs to support its people.

the argument that international economic integration maximizes world output ignores basic causal factors

The orthodox economics emphasizes "the optimal allocation of resources" in an economy as a factor affecting its efficiency. In keeping with its emphasis on equilibrium, this economic theory conventionally assumes that the quantity of resources and the conditions of production are given and fixed. It also assumes that the only people importantly affected by economic deals are those who decide the deals. Applying this set of assumptions, the conclusion reached—with exceptions depicted as minor—is that "the optimal allocation of resources" occurs when government and public policy do not intrude, but leave matters to be settled by the self-serving actions of individuals and firms. That this theory does not describe the situation that actually exists or explain the actual performances of economies has been pointed out through past decades by many varieties of critics.

This version of economics interprets international trade by applying its conventional set of assumptions. The question asked is, "Assuming that resources and conditions of production are fixed and the interests reflected in private transactions are the only ones that need be considered, what is the best way of managing international trade?" The answer, given the way the question is posed, is not surprising: unregulated transactions, "free trade."

But, in actuality, international trade can importantly affect all of the things that the orthodox economics takes as independently given and fixed. International economic integration affects population, and thus living standards in the nations involved. Through this it affects the kinds of goods for which there is a market and the kinds of activities societies can support. Through these causal channels and others, it affects the technology and methods of production that are relevant and that nations can use. International trade thus can alter all of the fundamental conditions of economic life.

Thus the story told by the orthodox economics, in which international trade has no important indirect effects and only improves the details of use of fixed resources within a fixed context—and therefore free trade is the best arrangement—this story is really of no interest at all. It has no applicability to the situation that actually exists. It tells us nothing about the consequences that actually will follow any set of international economic policies. The causal relations and the events that actually dominate the outcome, and determine the fates of nations, are mainly left out of account in this kind of theory. Realism thus requires treating the subject in a basically different way.

the conventional argument that international trade increases "efficiency" is based on a false interpretation of efficiency

It commonly is argued that trade across national boundaries—like other trade—must be a source of efficiency, of gain; otherwise it would not occur. In a typical example used to support the argument, chilly Scotland grows oats. Sunny Spain grows oranges. They exchange a part of their specialized outputs, to their mutual advantage. This kind of case is taken to show that trade increases *efficiency*. Thus, barriers to trade damage efficiency, and are to be avoided. And thus, free trade is the best possible arrangement.

A difficulty with this interpretation is that not all cases fit its illustrative pattern. What of a case in which, say, low Spanish wages cause *nearly all kinds of goods* to be produced cheaper in Spain than in Scotland? Scottish goods are generally undersold by Spanish goods. Spanish industries expand and Spanish jobs increase on the basis of production for the Scottish market. Scottish industries shrink or fail and Scottish workers become unemployed. Scotland has a large deficit in its international payments. To balance its international payments and put its people back to work, Scotland sooner or later has to begin to match the low Spanish wage rates. It must undertake to reduce its standard of living to the Spanish level.

Is what Spain offers to Scotland in this exchange "efficiency"? In a certain sense, it is. Does not "efficiency" mean, "producing goods cheap"? And is not producing goods with low-wage labor a way of producing them cheaply? Is not, indeed, the ultimate "efficiency" the production of goods using workers who require nothing but the barest essentials of food, clothing, and shelter to keep them alive? Is it not, then, reasonable that the nation that can provide people who work on those terms will outcompete others because of its "efficient" production?

But, one is moved to object, this is not a kind of "efficiency" that serves human purposes. Though it is efficient in a certain narrow sense, arranging for goods to be produced by people who live at the lowest possible level is not the goal of economies.

It is, *other things unchanged*, advantageous to Scots to be able to buy cheap Spanish goods. But for Scots to buy the cheap Spanish goods cannot leave *other things unchanged*. It means they are not buying Scottish goods. And the Spaniards are not buying the expensive Scottish goods. If Scotland is going to buy cheap goods from Spain, in order to balance its international payments and permit its people to earn an income Scotland also is going to have to *sell goods to Spain*. The benefits of buying goods produced by cheap labor thus carry with them the problem that you must sell goods to the cheap-labor nation. This implies that your workers must compete with its cheap labor. The basic way to do this by also becoming cheap labor, by adjusting to lower wage rates and a lower standard of living.

In a broad sense, the "efficiency" that is desired from an economy involves "supporting high wage rates and a high standard of living for the people," not "producing goods cheap by having low wage rates and a low standard of living." The two kinds of "efficiency" are the opposite of one another. It is not surprising that they call for opposite policies.

"Efficiency," it seems, is a concept of many meanings, which needs to be used with care. Just as it is necessary to ask, "Competition *at what?*" it is essential to ask, "Efficiency *at what?*" From the viewpoint of a firm, it is efficient to produce with cheap labor. From the viewpoint of a buyer, it is efficient to buy goods that are cheap because they were produced with cheap labor. But it is not a goal of the nation to reduce its people to the status of providers of cheap labor.

To create and preserve a civilized, high-income society requires "efficiency"—if that term is to be applied—in a broader sense than is conceived of in prevailing economic theory. This is "efficiency" at creating and protecting a coherent and workable *economic system* that generates a high standard of living. Over time, it is efficiency in structuring evolutionary processes so that they take the society toward the desired kind of life. Developments that in some narrow or technical sense seem to comprise "efficiency" do not necessarily take the society in a constructive direction. They may even ruin it. Technically, nuclear weapons are a great achievement. Surely they are wonderfully "efficient" in some senses. But nuclear weapons are not necessarily "efficient" in elevating the quality of human life. They may prove to be wonderfully efficient at destroying it.

In the complex system of accomplishments that is required to make a civilized, high-income society, one essential kind of accomplishment is the avoidance of overpopulation and standards-lowering competition. In precluding this accomplishment, international economic integration—despite its "efficiencies" in narrower senses—could prove to be the undoing of advanced societies.

the basic requirement for constructive international trade is that it be balanced, and on terms that bring benefit to each of the nations involved

Technical "efficiency" and "cheapness" thus are not reliable guides to what pattern of international trade is beneficial to a nation, or what pattern of international trade benefits mankind in general. What, then, is the condition that must be met if a nation is to benefit from international trade? A key condition is that the nation's trade (or trade plus other sustainable international payments) must be *in balance*. When this condition is met, the nation assuredly avoids the position of buying goods abroad but being unable to sell abroad, and thus avoids being forced to lower its wage rate and standard of living in order to meet foreign competition. If the nation's trade is in balance, then industries and jobs are not, on balance, being shifted from its economy to the economy of some other nation.

If the nation's trade is in balance, and if the over-all package of trade, considering its indirect as well as its direct effects, is beneficial to the nation, then all is well. *That* is the condition that needs to be met for international trade to have a constructive effect on the economic welfare of nations and peoples.

This point was emphasized in economics before the rise of faith in natural harmony and *laissez faire*. Adam Smith ridiculed this conception. He asserted that the nation did not need to worry that international trade, and the need to meet low-wage foreign competition, would force down its wage rates and its standard of living. Subsequent orthodox economics continued to make this claim. It seems that the orthodox economics is wrong about this. The earlier view was correct. Being thrown into competition with low-wage labor and low-standards production in other countries is a threat to the standard of living of a high-income nation.

The basic means of protecting against that hazard is for each nation to assure that its trade is balanced, and balanced on terms that benefit the nation. In determining what it views as "benefit," each nation must define and apply its goals, and effectuate its interpretation of what comprises economic improvement. The nation must provide its knowledge, its analysis, its interpretation as to what policy actions and arrangements will be required actually to cause the kind of outcome it desires. These essential inputs of defined human goals and of knowledge and analysis must necessarily underlie any rational, responsible policy toward international trade. In a cause-and-effect world, there is no way to get what you want except by knowing what you want, and knowing what actions will cause you to get it. And for international trade in today's world, there is no entity that can act effectively on behalf of people except national governments.

under different circumstances, international trade can damage high-wage nations or low-wage nations

In the early nineteenth century, the complaint most widely raised against unregulated international trade was that it caused less developed nations to be damaged by low-cost imports from the experienced industries of England, which prevented them from developing their industries and providing rewarding jobs for their people. A case emphasized in this book seems to be the opposite of this one. Low-wage nations undersell the manufactured goods of the high-wage, industrialized, Western nations, and take their industries away from them.

It may seem reasonable to react, "But these cases are the opposite of one another, so they cannot both be true. Is the *principle*, then, that industrialized nations undersell and damage underdeveloped nations, or that low-wage nations undersell and damage high-wage nations?"

This is not a rational response. There is no inconsistency in the two kinds of case. The effects of international trade depend on the joint operation of a number of causal factors. If one wishes a general rule or principle, it must be: "Low costs undersell high costs, and when one nation generally undersells another nation this causes a process of change that, depending on circumstances of the case, may be seriously damaging to one or both nations."

England in the early nineteenth century had well developed manufacturing industries, aggressive commercial tactics, and still low wage rates. Other nations had low, or lower, wage rates, but lacked the capability under unrestricted international trade of creating manufacturing firms that did not quickly succumb to British competition.

In recent decades, on the other hand, some nations with wage rates that are only a fraction of those of Western nations *do* have the capability to launch manufacturing operations that from the first can undersell Western firms. The difference in circumstances leads to a difference in outcome.

And there are, of course, more than these two kinds of case. Many nations today have little industry, and despite low wage rates have little capacity to start industries that can survive in the face of foreign competition. This kind of problem still exists. To treat international trade realistically requires accurately interpreting diverse situations and sets of causal factors, and many kinds of episodes and processes, on which the fortunes of nations depend.

Interpreting International Trade Within the Thought-World of Modern Science

International trade assumes a quite different appearance when considered within the system of ideas of modern science than when viewed within the natural-harmony framework that still governs the orthodox economic theory. Two different views emerge of the existing situation of the nations and trade, and of the directions in which events could move. The hazards that are to be avoided and the kinds of policies that are reasonably considered are quite different in the two views. What is at stake is not a mere matter of words, or of intellectual style or fashion. Past experience shows the decisive importance of the structuring of human activities, and shows specifically how greatly, and how surprisingly, international trade can alter the powers, the wealth, the fates of nations. To deal with this subject and the related policies effectively in the radically changed world of the late twentieth century is one of the great challenges of the times.

3

Effects of International Trade

Whether an action will be harmful or beneficial depends on the effects it will have. Not many actions have only a single effect. Even a carefully planned action, such as taking a prescribed dose of medicine, can have several different kinds of effects. Unwanted effects that come along with the desired ones are often called "side effects."

International trade necessarily has "side effects" that come along with its desired effects. To design reasonable policies on international trade requires taking account of all of the effects of policy actions, the bad with the good, the indirect with the direct, the long-term with the short-term, the nonobvious with the obvious. This chapter considers some of the different kinds of effects of trade across national boundaries that need to be taken into account in estimating the consequences of policies toward international trade.

The term, "international trade," taken literally, means "trade between nations," as nations, just as "international relations" means "relations between nations as represented by their governments." It requires active effort to remember that what actually is meant by "international trade" is "trade that crosses national boundaries." Ordinarily this trade is not negotiated between governments, or between "nations" as nations. Rather it is carried out by private parties in pursuit of their private interests. In many cases, these parties would be residents of one the countries in question, but there is no necessity that they should be. Trade between the United States and Taiwan, for example, could be carried out by a Japanese firm. To help keep the distinction in mind, trade between nations, arranged by their governments, can be called "internation" trade, rather than "international" trade.

Potential Gains from International Trade

How might internation trade or international trade be beneficial to the nations that engage in it? Several bases of a potential for mutual gain to nations (to nations, as distinguished from the private parties involved) can be noted.

First, nations in many cases differ in the things they are good at, in their climates or natural resources. Under these circumstances, if each nation specializes in the things it does best, and they exchange, there is a potential for arranging a deal in which both nations benefit. Grow the wheat on the American prairie and the bananas in tropical Latin America, and strike a deal that makes both nations better off than they would be if each nation tried to grow both things.

A second basis of potential gains to nations from international trade applies especially to small nations. Some goods can be produced efficiently only on a large scale, in giant, specialized plants. That is true of automobiles, aircraft, steel, and to some degree of many products. A large nation may have a domestic market big enough to support giant, efficient automobile plants, say, on the basis of its domestic market.

But a small nation will not be able to do this. It can gain the efficiencies of large-scale production only by tying into the market of a large nation or a group of nations. To do this, it must specialize in some small number of goods, and import many of the goods it needs from other nations. Thus, for some decades Switzerland specialized in producing watches and in its tourist industry. Through these, it paid for the many kinds of goods it imported from other nations, which it could not efficiently have produced at home. The operation of this factor makes large nations generally less dependent on international trade than are small ones.

Another factor tending to make a nation dependent on international trade is a low standard of living. The home market of a nation with a low standard of living is largely limited to the goods that people with small incomes can buy. Moreover, a low-income society lacks the economic base to support advanced education and research, large investment, first-class electric power, railroads, and communications. So the kinds of goods it is capable of producing—unless foreign firms or multinational corporations enter the picture—are limited.

For these reasons, the low-income country commonly is unable to produce efficiently many things that it needs: medicines and drugs, machinery, fertilizer, trucks, aircraft, automobiles. It must rely on importing such things from countries that are in a position to produce them efficiently. If it were cut off from the outside world, its situation would in some cases be disastrous. Even with these goods available from other nations, the low-income country, depending on its specific circumstances and its raw materials, may have great difficulty generating enough exports to pay for its required imports.

One final kind of basis for mutually beneficial international trade is the differences in the positions of nations with reference to particular natural resources. For example, some nations have no oil deposits within their borders, while others have much more oil than they can use, but have little else to sustain them. This also is the case with coal, and with metals. Warm, sunny beaches or attractive mountains can play a similar role, since nations that possess them can pay for their imports by taking care of tourists from nations that lack them. Accidents of circumstance that give nations very different endowments of scarce natural resources thus are another potential basis for international or internation trade that benefits both nations.

An important point that emerges from considering the bases of international trade is how different are the positions of various nations in relation to international trade. The large, high-income nation with a full range of natural resources may have little need of international trade. The United States and the Soviet Union are in somewhat this position.

At the other extreme, small nations like Switzerland and Denmark are heavily dependent on international trade to permit them to get the benefits of specialized, large-scale production and to sustain the high standard of living to which they are accustomed. Other nations are heavily dependent on a small number of nations that are in the forefront of work in science, technology, and applied knowledge of many types. They essentially follow along behind the leading nations, buying or copying the fruits of their achievements.

In the degree of their dependence on international trade, and in the particular kinds of things they require from other nations and the particular kinds of things they have to sell, thus, the various nations are in widely different positions. The simple illustrations and purportedly universal "principles" in terms of which international trade often is considered do not bring out that in relation to international trade the various nations have different needs, different things to gain, and different things to lose.

The Effects of International Trade; An Illustrative Case

The pattern of its international trade has many effects on a nation. Some of these work out in complex ways, and are not at all obvious. The outcome can depend on interaction among a number of causal factors, or on the role of causal factors that operate conditionally, that apply in one case or one period of time but not in another. A realistic analysis of the effects of international trade, and of the implications of policies toward international trade, must take account of all of these different kinds of effects. It is useful to begin consideration of this challenging task by looking at an illuminating illustrative case.

Is international trade now causing the "deindustrialization" of the United States?[1] This question has been the basis of much recent discussion and controversy. The present situation of the United States and the West lends special interest to a much earlier, and very thorough-going, case of deindustrialization, the decline of the North Italian towns in the early seventeenth century. Carlo Cipolla describes the process:

> Dutch, English, and French products ousted Italian products not only from foreign markets, but also from the Italian one. The combined loss of foreign and internal markets brought about a drastic collapse of production and a massive disinvestment in the manufacturing and service sectors. . . . In Cremona in 1615 there were one hundred eighty-seven firms producing woolens . . . By 1749 only two firms were in business. . . .
>
> The fundamental reason for the replacement of Italian goods and services by foreign ones was always basically the same: English, Dutch, and French commodities and services were offered at lower prices. . . .
>
> What had happened to Italy is a good example of the ambivalence of foreign trade. From the eleventh to the sixteenth centuries foreign trade had been indeed an "engine of growth" for Italy . . . From the beginning of the seventeenth century, however . . . the structure of Italian foreign trade changed completely. Foreign manufactures were brought in and drove Italian products and their manufacturers out of the market. At the same time foreign demand favored the production of oil, wine, and raw silk. One may argue that in the short run Italy derived from this new arrangement some comparative advantages of the kind illustrated by the Ricardian theory. In the long run, however, foreign trade acted as an "engine of decline": it contributed to shift both capital and labor from the secondary and tertiary sectors to agriculture. In regard to labor this shift meant, in the long run, a) the reduction in number of both the literate craftsmen and the enterprising merchants, b) the growth in size of the illiterate peasantry, and c) the

rise in power of the landed nobility. . . . The cities lost their previous vitality. The great Universities of Padua and Bologna slipped into oblivion. Venice sent her best gunfounder, Alberghetti, to London to learn the most modern techniques for working metals. The few remaining Italian clockmakers copied the style and the mechanisms of the numerous and skillful London clockmakers. Italy had begun her career as an underdeveloped area within Europe.[2]

As interpreted by Cipolla, the major factors that caused the undercutting of Italian manufacturers by foreign ones were Italy's higher wage rates, excessive and poorly conceived taxation, excessive control of production methods by the guilds, and the failure of the Italians to match the lower quality and lower priced goods designed by the Dutch and English.[3] These factors have their counterparts in the present-day world.

Some Points Illustrated by this Case

Italy's economic decline is by no means atypical. Most historical cases of rapid economic rise and decline of nations have centered around a changing pattern of the nation's international trade, which altered the goods the nation exported and imported, and thus the particular industries in which it could specialize and the kinds of production in which it was able to engage. Thus the points drawn from the illustrative case of seventeenth-century Italy are potentially applicable to international trade in general. They need to be considered in relation to the recent shift in the pattern of trade of the United States and the West, and the associated shift in the kinds of production in which these nations will be able to engage, and the kinds of jobs they will offer to their people.

the pattern of international trade determines which industries are located in which countries

The economic rise and the later fall of the Italian towns resulted from shifts in the pattern of international trade, and the changes these caused in the location of industries in various countries. Italy was raised up to a high standard of living and a position of economic leadership as it took over international manufacture of woolens (as well as banking, and some other activities).

When the area's textile manufacturing industry was undercut by foreign production, the pattern of trade changed, and the region became an importer rather than an exporter of textiles. It suffered an economic decline that was the counterpart of its earlier rise. The shift in the pattern of international trade and in the international location of industries was the central causal factor in both events. The loss of industries that were a major foundation of their economic position and standard of living is a feature shared by the North Italian towns in this illustrative episode, and—on a less extreme scale, at least so far—the United States and other Western nations in recent experience.

different industries have different effects on the economic status and economic prospects of a nation

In the world picture painted by individualistic economics, in which international trade is automatically self-regulating, it appears that one industry is as good as another. If a nation loses some industries, it will automatically gain others—though just how and when this occurs is glossed over. The implication is that the new industries gained necessarily will be at least as good as the ones that were lost. Otherwise—recall that this economics asserts international trade to be automatically beneficial to each of the nations involved—otherwise the shift of industries could not have occurred in the first place. This version of economics also does not indicate what automatic mechanism exists that could prevent nonbeneficial shifts in international trade from occurring.

Experience obviously does not conform to this pattern. The shift from agriculture to manufacturing raised up the North Italian towns, made them world leaders. The return to agriculture doomed them to economic decline—a decline whose effects in this case lasted for centuries.

At any particular time, it seems, certain industries are especially rewarding. These industries make winners of the nations in which they are located. In the seventeenth century, such rewarding industries included textile manufacturing, shipping and the carrying out of international trade, and international banking. In the late twentieth century, other industries will prove to be the winner-makers. These industries permit a nation to earn high incomes and support a high standard of living. In some cases, they also make for a self-perpetuating position of leadership by conferring skills and knowledge that then keep the nation ahead of others.

At any time there are other lines of production that doom a nation to economic backwardness and a low standard of living, to economic failure. They do not provide a high standard of living—with all the indirect benefits and potentialities for cumulative advance it confers. They have no future; they lead only to continued failure. In the seventeenth century and earlier, for the nation's people to be largely engaged in subsistence agriculture or peasant agriculture was the mark of, and source of, economic failure.

England had risen from subsistence agriculture in the fifteenth century in a cumulative movement that was to make that little nation the economic leader of the world, a position it held into the nineteenth century. In the episode discussed, England took one of its economic steps upward, and Italy took a decisive step downward—toward a backward state from which that region was not fully to recover until recent decades.

In international trade and the location of industries, some nations must be winners and others losers

Economics textbooks have argued that international trade is beneficial to all nations, and have ridiculed the idea that one nation's gain may be another nation's loss. But experience shows that in international trade and the international location of rewarding industries one nation's gain is necessarily another nation's loss. During the era when textile manufacturing was the leading industry, the cutting edge of economic progress, the nation that gained the industry was made a winner. The nation that lost it was the loser.

The situation of nations competing for the most rewarding industries closely parallels that of individuals who are competing for the most attractive jobs. There are at in any particular set of circumstances only so many of these attractive jobs. For one person to get one means that another person does not get it.

It is not necessarily clear in advance which industries, or which occupations, will make winners and which will make losers. But there obviously is no mechanism that makes all industries or occupations equally advantageous. Experience shows that some offer very high rewards and others low ones. Obviously, no mechanism exists to assure that a nation that fails to gain an attractive industry will be awarded another one that is no less attractive. The set of industries that exists at any point in time includes some winner-makers and some loser-makers. The pattern of international trade and international location of industries determine which nations will be cast in the role of winners, and which ones will be the losers.[4]

the international location of industries depends on national policies and institutions

The "free trade" doctrine asserts that a nation should accept whatever industries come its way, as determined by "competition" and "the free market." It claims that this arrangement is neutral as among nations, and leads to "the optimum allocation of world resources." "Competition" and "the free market" are depicted as unquestionably valid judges. What they decree is *what ought to be*. They reflect basic and valid forces and principles, and make no errors.

But experience shows that the shifts of industries between nations that cause the rise of one nation and the fall of another often depend not on basic, valid, and inexorable forces but upon temporary and accidental conditions, and on differences in the current policies and institutions of the nations involved. A nation can be put on an evolutionary path that imposes on it centuries of economic backwardness by mere accidental or transitory factors, or by its temporarily unfavorable laws or policies. What happens is not "what has to be," and is not necessarily "what ought to be."

The record of experience shows that differences in national economic policies and institutions, as well as temporary circumstantial factors, always have played a major role in determining which nations gained the winning industries and became economic successes. In the illustrative case discussed above, the economic failure of the North Italian towns was not predetermined by Nature, but was caused by policy actions and institutional factors: the high Italian wage rates, the influence of the guilds over production methods and the kinds of cloth that were produced, the excessively high and ill-designed taxes, and the unsettled political conditions in Italy.

On the other side, England's extraordinary economic rise depended at each step on supportive government actions and on institutions and behavior patterns that were developed so as to contribute to England's take-over of the rewarding industries of the times. The low English wage rates at that point in time were a significant factor in the process. The same was true of the rise of the Netherlands, and of France.[5]

The nations whose economic failure was the other side of English success from the seventeenth to the nineteenth centuries were struck by the extent to which the outcome depended on the toughness, or the unscrupulousness, of the English campaign to undersell all actual and potential competitors. In their view, the outcome depended less on a judicial decree from "the free market" than on the power of the British fleet, the British control of the markets of their colonies, and the harsh tactics of the British government and British merchants. Portugal's economic prospects were ruined by its notorious Methuen Treaty with England. England's use of power to force its opium trade on China is an extreme illustration.[6] Actions by governments in recent years to influence the pattern of international trade and gain desired industries and jobs—the influencing of exchange rates, assisting and subsidizing of favored export industries, hidden or devious discouragements of undesired imports—are not new to the world.

Experience shows that the course of international trade reflects no objective and omniscient mechanism whose doings are above question—so that what happens is just what should happen. Quite the contrary. The lesson is that in this area nothing is predetermined. Perhaps, if temporary political factors had pushed events onto a different track, Italy might have remained the world economic leader. With different institutions and government actions, England might have remained a backward little island living off its acorn-fed pigs. Amsterdam might have remained a desolate town sitting on its mud flat. "The free market" could have led as readily to one as to the other of those outcomes.

Which of the potential outcomes became the actual one depended critically on the policies, the institutions, the behaviors of the societies involved, and on purely temporary and accidental factors that can put events on one path rather than another. Thus, that England rose to world economic dominance and that Italy declined to economic backwardness did not reflect *basic* and *permanent* factors. Rather, the economic fates of these nations were determined by cumulative economic processes that at decisive points were governed by temporary government policies, institutional factors, and accidental events that in no way validated, or required, the path that events actually took. Mankind might have been as well off, or better off, had these temporary factors put economic history on quite a different path. And the economic future, like the past, is quite open to the influence of temporary factors, and of wise and foolish, realistic and unrealistic, national policies.

the capabilities of societies are affected by shifts in international trade

A shift in the pattern of international trade causes shifts of industries among countries. The change in industries and occupations alters the character of the societies and their processes of economic improvement or economic decline. Again, the case of the North Italian towns illustrates the point. The economic rise of these towns created demands for new kinds of production, new occupations, and new skills. It provided the means of financing the development of factories and equipment. It made of the towns and their people something they had not been before.

The loss of the markets for the towns' new industries, which underlay their new standard of living and their new occupations and skills, reversed this process. The factories were idled. They decayed. The skills of the people were forgotten and lost, as they no longer were in demand and could not be used. Those people whose jobs had disappeared faded back into the countryside or moved to other areas. The export trade built the towns into something they had not been before, with capabilities they had not possessed. The loss of the markets, the jobs, the skilled occupations, and the high incomes reversed all of this. The area slid backward down the slope it earlier had ascended.

Dramatic illustrations of the positive transformation of societies by international trade are provided by England and the Netherlands during the periods in which they were moving into possession of the leading industries of the times. "At the end of the fifteenth century, England was an 'underdeveloped country'—underdeveloped not only by comparison with the modern industrialized countries, but also in relation to the standards of the 'developed' countries of that time, such as Italy, the Low Countries, France, and Southern Germany. . . . At the middle of the sixteenth century, England looked very different from what she had been half a century earlier. By 1550, England was a prosperous, dynamic country, a country which was lining up with the most advanced countries in Europe of the time."[7]

The transformation of England into a society with capabilities not dreamed of in the earlier period was caused by the nation's step-by-step acquisition of new and rewarding industries based on international trade. In doing this, England necessarily displaced other nations from these progress-making industries—commercialized wool-growing, the manufacture of cloth and of textile products, shipping and trade, the manufacture of products from iron. The increase in incomes, in skills and accomplishments, in orientation towards technical innovation and "being number one" were essential elements in the rise of

England to a position of general economic and industrial leadership of the world.

With each step in this process, England became something different from what it had been before. The capabilities and characteristics of its people, the size of its population, its standard of living and the kinds of occupations it could support, its orientation, interests, social structure, even its "resources" in the practical sense of "resources as these are used." Virtually nothing was unaffected by the transformation of the society that was caused by the shift in its industries and the pattern of its international trade.

The process of economic rise is a cumulative or self-feeding one, an evolutionary one. One step creates the capability of taking another step, which earlier would have been impossible. And the process works in both directions. As new capabilities can be developed, old ones can be lost. Understanding the effects of international trade requires understanding these cumulative processes of economic rise and fall with which it is inseparably connected. An interpretation of international trade that does not take account of its influence on such cumulative processes cannot be realistic.

The evolutionary processes of the decades that now lie ahead will modify the character and capabilities of the various nations, raising some upward, pushing others downward, and bringing economic betterment or deterioration to nations in general. As was true in the past, the direction of these economic processes is not predetermined. It will depend on accidents, circumstances, on the actions and policies of national governments—and on the knowledge and wisdom, the errors and the delusions, that lie behind them.

A challenging question thus is: "What will the United States and the other Western nations *be*, say, thirty years from now? What will be their capabilities, their powers? To what new heights will they have been carried by the evolutionary processes of the decades ahead, or how far will they have fallen from the way of life that was theirs in the decades after the Second World War?

International Trade in Processes of Economic Rise and Decline of Nations

In a cause-and-effect world, any event is determined by, and explained by, a set of causal factors. An event then changes the existing situation and thus affects the set of factors that determine the next event. Events thus move ahead through time in a chain-reaction or evolutionary way.

Interpreting an event correctly requires a framework for taking account of all of the causal factors that combine to determine it. It is necessary to analyze the way different types of causal factors interact with one another and combine to determine events, and to understand the kinds of self-feeding evolutionary processes that shape human affairs and the rise and decline of nations. In dealing with living systems such as societies and peoples, we must keep in mind, everything is subject to change over time; nothing is fixed, unchangeable, or predetermined.

The evolutionary processes affecting societies are sensitive to the way human affairs are structured. Different degrees and forms of international economic integration imply different structures of human organization, and different kinds of evolutionary processes, working toward different outcomes. We consider now some ways in which the economic role of the nation and the form of international economic integration affect the evolutionary processes that will shape human life in the decades ahead.

the potential for cumulative increases in living standards

For a nation to achieve a higher standard of living brings about a new situation, in which it has some additional potentialities for further economic advance. Through a number of causal links, economic improvement can be a cumulative or self-feeding process. An increase in its wage level and standard of living can give the nation an increased ability to:

develop a large domestic market for advanced goods such as automobiles and aircraft, electronic equipment, and computers, which permit the nation to use advanced technology in its production;

support an expensive system of advanced training and education that qualifies its people to use advanced technology and production methods;

develop and maintain first-rate services such as electricity, telephone, airlines, railroads, banking and finance;

support through taxation a government that provides high quality services and makes a favorable climate for efficient economic activities;

gain through its exports any materials that are needed for production and are not available domestically;

engage in research and development programs that permit it to become a world leader in rewarding lines of production and thus earn high incomes by escaping from low-income lines of production;

engage in large-scale saving, productive investment, and capital formation.

These causal factors, under conditions that are favorable in other respects, can feed a cumulative process of economic improvement in a society. They can cause "positive-feedback loops" in which one improvement makes for further improvements ("positive" because the effect goes in the same direction as the cause). Such self-feeding processes of economic advancement are the basis of the economic success stories that have set the pattern for human hopes and expectations.

The structure of this kind of interaction-system, in which a number of causal factors interact to determine the course of events, is depicted in Figure 3-1. The diagram shows how the first of the factors just listed could fit into a self-feeding process of economic improvement. The same kind of diagram could be drawn for each of the other factors listed. Actual processes of

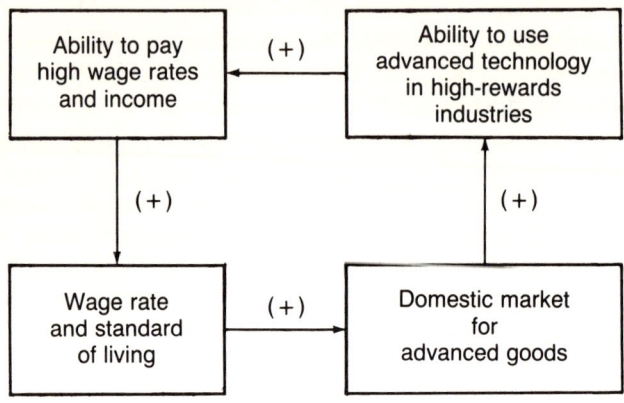

**Figure 3-1
Interaction-Process Contributing
to Economic Advancement**

economic improvement ordinarily involve many such jointly acting feedback loops.

It would be possible also to draw a diagram to depict all these loops and all the causal linkages among the factors involved in a process of economic rise. To knowledgeable experts in the causal analysis of processes of economic change, such diagrams would be useful. The causal structures represented in such a diagram also could be embodied in computer simulation models. These would spell out quantitatively the different processes over time that would occur under various sets and structures of causal factors. Drawing such a diagram at this point in our discussion might be more confusing than helpful, but to trace in one's mind or in less comprehensive diagrams the various causal loops that are discussed is a useful exercise.

It must be kept in mind that the causal relations depicted are all conditional. That is, they operate in some cases, not in others, depending on circumstances and on national policies and institutions. An increase in the standard of living, for example, creates the potential for a nation to develop an improved and more advanced educational system. But in some cases this potential will not be realized. In other cases, more money may be spent on education but the schooling may be of a type that does more harm than good. Costly educational systems that are an economic liability rather than an asset are to be found in some countries.

In a case in which all of the causal relations depicted are operating to cause self-feeding improvement in living standards, the greater any of the responses is, the more rapid is the process of economic improvement. For example, the greater the effect of a rise in living standards in causing an improvement in the nation's educational system, the greater the feedback tending to accelerate the rise in the standard of living. The greater the number of factors contributing to such a positive-feedback system, the more strongly they are working, the more powerful their interactions, and the more rapid the responses, the more rapid the resulting process of change will be.

Such a system of positive-feedback loops can work either to cause economic advancement or in the opposite direction, to cause economic decline. When the standard of living is declining, the interaction-processes discussed will work to make the *economic decline* self-feeding. It is the same causal system, but operating in the opposite direction. For example, a decline in the standard of living will reduce the domestic market for advanced goods, thus reducing the nation's ability to produce advanced goods based on its home market, its ability to reap the rewards of using advanced technology, and thus its ability to maintain a high standard of living, and so on around the circuit again. The cumulative powers of processes of economic change can work in either direction. The popularity of the idea that "progress" is natural, as is "economic growth" or "economic development," causes the potential for cumulative economic decline to be ignored or denied. But the actual experiences of nations provide abundant examples of such cumulative processes of economic deterioration.

The direction taken by such cumulative processes of economic rise or decline depends on the pattern of international trade. As has been seen, international trade and the shift of the rewarding industries to a particular country can contribute to causing that country's economic rise—and have the opposite effect on the countries from which these industries move. Another possible pattern is a general economic integration of nations through international trade, which keeps all of the nations near the same economic level. When the overriding factor determining this economic level is the existence of overpopulation in some parts of the world, the effect of international trade in this case is to impose poverty on all nations. The conditions under which international trade will have one or another effect, and the processes by which these effects occur, need further consideration.

markets for advanced goods; who gains the advantage of them?

Most cases of striking national economic advancement involved a particular pattern of international trade. A nation raised itself and gained a position of economic leadership by taking over a dominant position in leading and rewarding industries, and this *was based on its tapping of the markets for advanced goods of other countries*. The North Italian towns, we recall, rose to their temporary position of economic eminence by developing textile manufacturing, banking, and other industries based primarily on foreign markets. That is to say, their process of economic advancement was not based on producing for the home market, which was too small to support such economic advancement, but for the markets of other countries.

Other nations at that time were fully aware of the rewards for winning dominance in the international market for the goods produced by leading industries. Thus the competition for these markets was rough, even brutal. When the Italian towns lost these markets and England and other countries gained them, the results revealed again the critical importance of the pattern in which the nation engages in large-scale production of rewarding, advanced goods for the markets of other countries. This was the pattern of the Netherlands in its hour of economic glory, of England into the nineteenth century, of Venice, and in modern times of Japan, Taiwan, South Korea, Singapore, Hong Kong—all of the most striking success stories of rapid modern economic rise.

Some nations achieved a substantial degree of economic success that did not depend on the control of foreign markets. These were large nations: Ancient China, Russia and later the Soviet Union, and, of course, the United States. In the last case, other special factors were also operating, such as the unique ratio of land and resources to people, and the boost given to the nation's economic position by the two World Wars.

As among a group of nations that all are equally dependent on international trade, there is potentially a symmetry in the competition of nations to gain the most rewarding industries. A problem with this kind of case, however, is its potential for causing degenerative competition among nations, a matter that is discussed below.

An additional issue or difficulty arises in the case of a large nation (or group of economically integrated nations) that has the capability for a self-feeding process of economic advancement based on its own market. This nation does not need to base its economic advancement on the exploitation of foreign markets for advanced goods. It does not need to enter into competition with other nations for markets for advanced goods, under rules that may be damaging to it. For such a nation to permit its markets to be exploited by other nations, and for it thus to give up its potential for a domestically based process of self-feeding economic improvement would seem to be contrary to its interests.

From the viewpoint of a nation in this position, to permit other nations to tap its markets and take over its promising industries as the basis for *their* economic advancement is to acquiesce in a parasitic relation. The large nation would be permitting the potential benefits of its resource—the large market for advanced goods that was created by its size and its high standard of living—to be exploited by others for their advantage, rather than exploiting it for its own advantage.

It does not appear that this is reasonable behavior for a nation. Self-sacrifice, or throwing away one's advantages, is not a formula for success and survival in a cause-and-effect world. Conceivably the large nation could make the access of other nations to its domestic market for advanced goods an element in some larger deal that would, all things considered, benefit both nations. But for a nation that has created within its border a large market for advanced goods, and thus has created the basis for a self-feeding process of economic advancement, simply to give away this resource, permitting it to be used by other nations for their economic advancement, and even acquiescing in its own decline, is a self-destructive pattern of behavior.

The recent behavior of the United States and the West has included such a self-destructive element. The actions presumably reflected not a hidden death wish so much as an intellectual deficiency. Thinking about the matter only in terms of simple slogans and unrealistic theories—and buoyed by faith in "the principle of comparative advantage"—the United States and the West have been blind to effects of their policies.

The importance of historical, and recent, cases of outstanding economic advancement of nations based on the exploitation of the markets of other nations for advanced goods calls for careful consideration of the implications of this structure of international trade. This is the more true in that this pattern of events underlies the present economic crisis and the uncertain economic future of the West.

poverty-causing factors that "travel" only through the migration of people

Under what conditions do poverty and low wage rates in one nation pose a threat to the high wage rates and high standard of living of another nation? What kinds of policies must a high-income nation adopt to avoid having its standard of living undermined by dealings with a low-income society?

In all cases, the standard of living of a high-income nation can be undermined by the migration of people from low-income nations. Where such immigration into high-income nations is permitted and actually occurs, these nations will tend to draw people from nations that have low incomes and high unemployment rates. This influx of people into nations that are already more densely populated than is economically desirable and thus are subject to worsening pollution, crowding, and resource scarcity will reduce their standards of living and reduce or eliminate their potential for future economic improvement.

One kind of special case requires some further consideration. Suppose the people who move to the high-income nation from low-income nations are not permitted—by policies, or, temporarily, by circumstances—to compete for whatever positions they wish, but are limited to the more menial and low-paid jobs? The new workers then take over these undesirable jobs. Within the enlarged economy, the natives assume the preferred jobs, and the newcomers the less desirable ones. The average wage rate and standard of living in the nation is lowered, but the incomes and standard of living of the natives is raised.

In this arrangement, the natives and the newcomers comprise two noncompeting groups within the same territory. The natives are better off—at least in a limited sense and temporarily—because of the arrival of the newcomers (on the condition that they do not have to compete with them for the same jobs). The newcomers are not as well off as the natives, but they are better off than they were back home in their low-income nation. This pattern is recognizable as the one that has existed with reference to the "guest workers" in a number of Northern European nations.

By limiting the size of the immigration, and by keeping the immigrants in low-level jobs, the natives avoid the adverse effects that would come from unlimited immigration and full competition of the newcomers for jobs held by the natives. The creation of a two-class society, with—in a particular sense—a "privileged" and an "unprivileged" class involves a number of negative features. Moreover, the arrangement is one that will be sustainable over time only if the high-income nation can define and enforce rules that will make it so. If the immigrants are permitted to become permanent residents, acquire political rights, and they or their children become able to compete freely for all kinds of jobs, the effects, after a lag, become the same as for ordinary immigration, tending to depress wage rates and the standard of living of the nation and its native population.

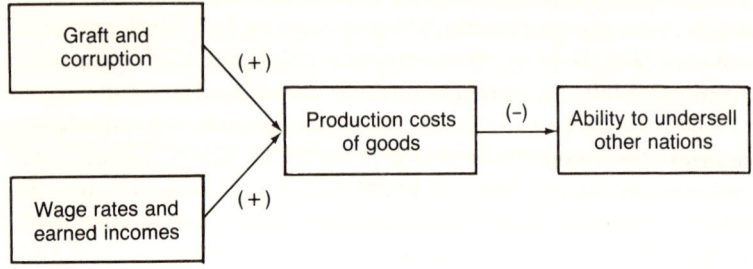

**Figure 3-2
Factors Affecting Production Costs and Ability
to Undersell Other Nations**

Some poverty-causing factors that can thus spread poverty to other nations through the movement of people, however, cannot thus spread poverty through the shipment of goods, through international trade. What are the defining characteristics of this kind of case?

This is a case in which the factors that impose poverty on the nation also make it an inefficient producer of goods and services. Thus, the ability to undersell goods produced in high-wage nations that the nation otherwise would have because of its low wages, it does not have because of its production inefficiency. The potential advantage in international trade of the low wage rates is offset by the nation's production inefficiency.

An illustration of the causal structure of this kind of case is given in Figure 3-2. In this case, the nation is afflicted with a custom of graft and corruption in government and business—which is an important problem in many nations. In relation to the nation's potential for a process of self-feeding economic improvement, this corruption factor imposes a negative-feedback loop that nullifies the positive factors that may be present and prevents the nation from achieving economic improvement.

The graft and corruption keep the economy in a condition of inefficient production, because of the unearned incomes they impose as costs of production, and because they prevent rational and realistic actions by government agencies and businesses. This production inefficiency causes a low wage rate and low standard of living. While the low wage rate, taken by itself, would give the nation a competitive advantage in foreign markets, the economic inefficiency that causes the low wage rate nullifies this potential advantage. Despite its low wage rate, the nation is unable to undersell producers in high-wage nations. It is not a threat to their industries, their jobs, their standard of living.

The existence of this condition is a matter of circumstances, which might change quickly. A reform government might wipe out the graft and corruption (though this is not an easy thing to do), thus quickly changing the economic position of the nation. With its efficiency improved but its wage rates still low, the nation now could threaten the position of high-wage nations by undercutting them in international trade. Another possible case is that in which, say, foreign firms manage to establish an enclave in which they escape from the ravages of graft and corruption, and thus provide a basis for the development of efficient, and still low-wage, production, and thus permit the nation to undersell high-wage nations.

But with these exceptions, low wage rates caused by factors that also cause production inefficiency pose little or no threat to high-wage nations because the disadvantage of their production inefficiency offsets the potential advantage of their low wage rates. Indeed, in such cases, international trade can be a serious threat to the already-unfavorable prospects of the low-wage nation. Its production inefficiency may more than offset the advantage of its low wage rates, so that goods from efficient high-wage nations undersell its goods, and outpace them in quality and variety. So it is the low-wage nation that finds itself with an intractable balance-of-payments deficit, running up foreign debts so long as foreigners will lend to it, and unable to balance its international trade through any feasible further reduction in its wage rates and living standards.

Among such poverty-causing factors that work by damaging the production capabilities of a nation are:

pervasive graft and corruption;

low intensity and quality of work;

inability to achieve effective, functional organizations;

pervasive disorder, violence, fear of breakdown of the nation's government;

extensive and disfunctional government regulations;

very high taxes (not offset by government services);

the power of a clique, a class, or labor groups to enforce unreasonable demands;

rivalries among political groups, leading to erratic and irrational government policies.

To some degree, such shortcomings are present in many societies, including high-income Western societies—some of which, indeed, may be in jeopardy because of increased strength of such factors. The low incomes of many societies of the world are explainable mainly in terms of one or more of these factors. Other societies do not have the level of incomes and economic achievement that their resources would permit because of these factors.

By causing economic inefficiency in the nation and thus making its standard of living low, these factors provide people an incentive to emigrate to nations that have high wage rates and available jobs. This movement of people is a threat to the standard of living in high-income nations. But in this type of case, the poverty of the low-income nations does not spread to high-income nations through international trade, but only through the movement of people.

overpopulation: the poverty-causing factor that "travels" through international trade

What of a nation that has a low wage rate and standard of living but suffers from none of these inefficiency-causing factors? It, then, *will* be in a position to undersell other nations and take their industries and their jobs from them. Its low wage rates will not be offset by production inefficiencies.

"But," one may ask, "if they have no such production inefficiencies, why do they have the low wage rates and living standard?" The answer is straightforward, "Because they are overpopulated, and the competition of people for jobs in the face of lack of land and resources can force the wage rate to a level that just sustains life—or even lower than this."

Because it causes low wage rates but does not, in itself, cause production inefficiencies, overpopulation in relation to a nation's resources is a poverty-causing factor that does "travel" through international trade. It provides a cost-advantage to production in the low-wage, overpopulated, nation that the high-wage nation does not—except in special cases—have any way to meet (other than by itself accepting low wage rates).

Thus, industries and jobs will tend to travel to the low-wage nation, and the product be shipped to the market of the high-wage nation. The effects of the overpopulation then "travel" to the high-wage nation, as it loses jobs and industries in relation to its population. This is another perspective on a matter discussed earlier—the tendency of international trade in this case to move the wage rates in the countries toward equality—thus, in effect, imposing the depressing effects of the overpopulation on both countries. The effects of the overpopulation thus "travel" to other countries through international trade.

international trade and the transmission of overpopulation-caused poverty to all nations

Population-growth and overpopulation has been a major poverty-causing factor throughout recorded history. Because of its ability to travel in various ways, and because of its potentially overwhelming force, overpopulation can dominate all other factors and force poverty on nations and, potentially, on all of mankind.

The generally optimistic economics of Adam Smith included the depressing theme that no matter how favorable other factors were, in a country with a high birth rate the growth of population eventually would cause a degree of overpopulation that would dominate the outcome and force low wage rates and a minimum standard of living. That is, the population factor would operate so powerfully as to nullify, after some lag, the factors that otherwise could have provided a positive transformation of the society and cumulative improvements in living standards.

The illustration that struck Adam Smith two hundred years ago was the China of his time. China had for many centuries been well organized, hard-working, and advanced in its production techniques. Yet it could not provide jobs for all of its people. Many lived at the border of starvation. The mortality rate, especially for children, was high. In production and work, China was at least as advanced as Europe, but its standard of living much lower. Why?

As Adam Smith saw, population growth there had caused a degee of overpopulation much greater than existed in Europe.[8] The same example can be used today. The Chinese government is aware that the nation's low standard of living and inability to provide enough productive jobs for its people is caused by overpopulation. The government has adopted severe measures to limit the birth rate and halt the growth of population.

An earlier section of this chapter discussed causal loops that potentially work to make economic improvement a self-feeding or cumulative process. A simple diagram to depict this kind of relation was given in Figure 3-1. How are these ways of thinking about processes of economic change to be applied to the factor, population-growth, with its possible result of overpopulation?

In nearly all countries now, an increase in population, unless offset by some other factor, acts to reduce the wage rate and lower the standard of living. Under these circumstances, if an increase in wage rates causes an increase in population, this leads to a negative-feedback loop. In this case, as is shown in Figure 3-3, an increase in the wage rate causes an increase in population, which then operates to cause a *reduction* in the wage rate.

With this causal linkage in operation, an increase in wage rates tends to be self-nullifying. This negative-feedback loop

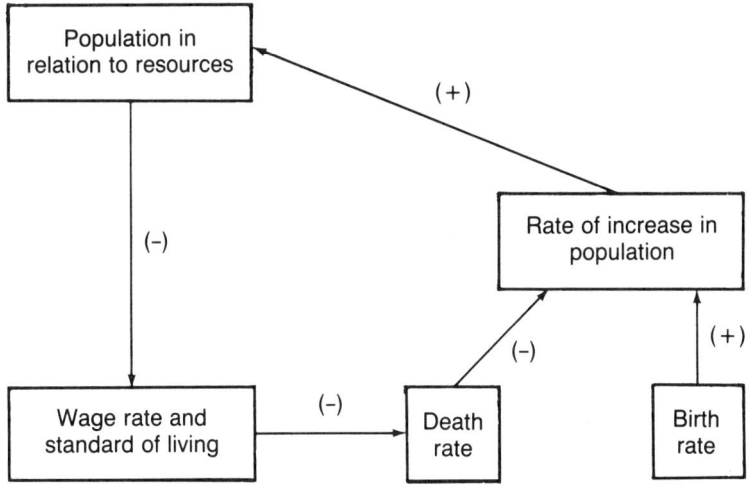

**Figure 3-3
Feedback Loop Involving Population
and Standard of Living**

thus will act to offset or counteract any positive-feedback loops that are operating to generate continued economic improvement. Given this reaction of population, favorable factors that otherwise would lead to a cumulative process of rise in the standard of living will cause an increase in population instead. In today's world, this is the great question! Which shall it be? An increase in living standards, or an increase in the number of people—and in the number of people living in poverty?

Earlier economics discussed this kind of question in terms of a causal interpretation of population-growth somewhat more detailed than has been considered here. In the kind of case that was taken for granted by Adam Smith and his contemporaries, and later analyzed by Malthus, the nation has a high birth rate and large family size. Thus, when the death rate of infants and youths is small and nearly all those born live to become parents, the population increases rapidly. Under these conditions, a human population can double in twenty years or less—as those of some nations have been doing recently.

But for the output of a nation—and particularly the output of food in an already-crowded nation—to double every twenty years is something that can occur only under special conditions. In other cases, the growth in population will outrun the increase in available food, other goods, and jobs, and will force down the wage rate and the standard of living.

When the basic wage level is forced down to a certain point, malnutrition and related increases in disease cause an increase in the death rate, especially that of infants and children. Thus, many of those who are born do not live to become parents. The high birth rate in this case does not imply a rapid increase in population, since it is offset by the high death rate.

The behavior generated by the nation with a high birth rate then is this. Whenever the standard of living is above some minimum level, which was termed "the subsistence level," the population increases rapidly. The resulting increase in population, after some lag, forces the standard of living downward. The population keeps increasing until the standard of living is forced down to the subsistence level, to the situation in which want and malnutrition are such as to raise the death rate to equality with the high birth rate, so that the population stabilizes. But in such a high-birth-rate society, the population is stable *only* under conditions of dire economic want and a high death rate. Under more favorable conditions, the population increases, which tends to drive the standard of living back down to the subsistence level.

The effect of this causal loop involving population, then, is not to make an increase in the standard of living self-feeding, but to make it self-reversing. In cases dominated by this causal loop, a favorable factor that raises the standard of living does not lead to a chain of interacting improvements in the nation's economic situation. Rather, it leads to an increase in its population. Since the increase in population prevents a lasting increase in the standard of living, all of the favorable causal links that could have operated if the standard of living had continued to

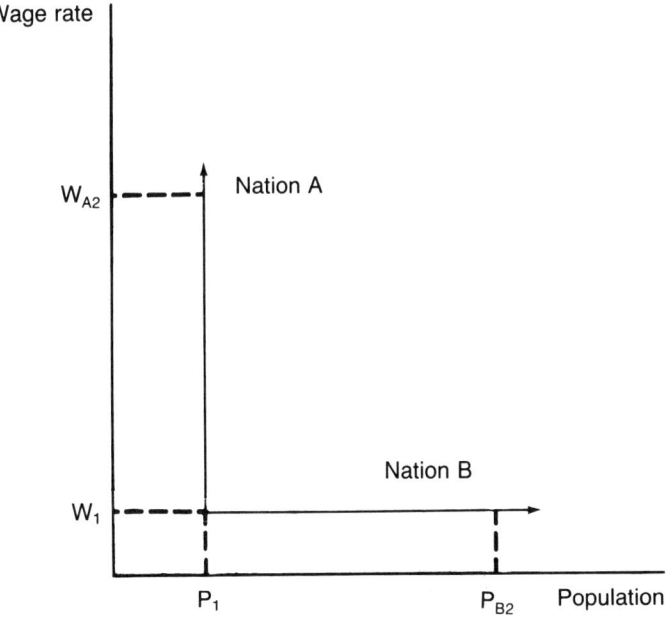

**Figure 3-4
Alternative Effects of Increase in National
Production Efficiency**

rise do not operate. Their potential positive effects do not come into operation.

The important role of the population factor illustrates how it is that different nations move along quite different evolutionary paths. Two nations that experienced a favorable development that increased their standards of living could then go on to two very different outcomes. In Nation A in Figure 3-4, the increase in the standard of living causes no increase in population because its initial birth rate was low. Then all of the positive causal links associated with an increased standard of living could work to bring about a cumulative process of economic improvement.

Nation B has a high birth rate, and makes the opposite response. The rise in its standard of living reduces its death rate and accelerates its population-growth. The rise in the population in time forces the standard of living back to the initial level. The causal chains that potentially could feed cumulative economic improvement, and that did so in Nation A, are prevented from operating. In this case, the final effect of the favorable disturbance is only to increase its population, with no increase in living standards. The experience of many countries, both in earlier times and in recent decades, corresponds to this unfavorable case. In these countries, improvements in knowledge and technology have been reflected in a multiplication of population, with little or no improvement in the standard of living.

These two cases thus illustrate the operation of different interaction-processes. The factor that determines which interaction-process applies to a nation is the birth rate of the nation, and the response of its population to a rise in the standard of living.

If Nation A and Nation B were combined, or were economically integrated by free movement of population or free trade, what would the outcome be? Raising this question brings to attention the unique causal role of population, which led earlier economics to make it the decisive factor in determining wage rates and living standards in the long run. The point is a strictly quantitative one. Human beings are quite capable of doubling their population in less than twenty years, generation after generation, even century after century. A population that increases by 3½ percent a year, as some now are doing, nearly doubles in twenty years. In fifty years, it increases more than fivefold; in a century, by more than 26 times; in a period of two centuries, 704 times.

In areas where unused fertile land, water, space, and resources do not exist, output of food and other goods cannot increase for long at such a pace. The numbers of people become excessive in relation to land, resources, space, and useful jobs. Enough productive work for all of them at wage rates that will support life cannot be found.

Thus the distinctive feature of population-growth as a causal factor is its *power*. It has the power potentially to overrule all other causal factors and dominate the outcome, forcing human poverty, want, and a high death rate.

This is a point that one understandably wishes were not true, and people have found many ingenious excuses for pretending it is not true. This argument is often offered: "Malthus was a pessimist. He said that the population always outgrows the food supply and causes poverty. But in many nations that has not happened. Therefore, Malthus is shown to be wrong. Therefore, there is no population problem."

What Malthus actually said is illuminating, and is all too well supported by subsequent experience. He pointed out the power of population-growth to dominate the human condition, but emphasized that population-growth was not predetermined, and that birth rates and family size differed widely among societies, depending heavily on social, institutional, and policy factors. His point was that a society could continue to enjoy a high standard of living for a protracted period of time only by preventing excessive population-growth, which it could do only by bringing about a sufficiently low birth rate and family size.

So the power of overpopulation to overrule other factors and enforce poverty becomes a critical factor determining the effects of international trade and international economic integration. As has been shown, a nation can fall victim by another nation's poverty, which is caused by *its* overpopulation. This can occur not only through the movement of people from the low-wage to the high-wage nation, but also through trade between the nations, through the movement of industries and jobs from high-wage nations to low-wage nations.[9]

The movement of either people or goods tends to equalize wage rates and living standards in different nations. The level at which this equalization occurs depends on the population, and the degree of overpopulation, of the world. Nations or regions that do not prevent population-growth—and preventing it is unusual—will contribute to causing poverty throughout the world.

The nation that is not overpopulated and not subject to population-growth can protect its economic future only by avoiding general economic integration with overpopulated nations. This requires limiting its immigration and assuring that its international trade is balanced, and on terms that are not damaging to it. The future success of mankind in general depends on some nations thus protecting themselves from the effects of overpopulation in other parts of the world, and preserving those human achievements and prospects that can be maintained only in societies that are not dominated by overpopulation and poverty.

Realistic consideration of the operation of interaction-processes such as govern the evolution and the fate of nations is a matter of some complexity, which must be approached within a suitable framework. There is no predetermined outcome. Many causal factors potentially are involved, their weights differing greatly among cases and time periods. Potential causal factors may or may not operate in a particular case, depending on side conditions. Important among these side conditions are social, institutional, political, and legal factors in the various nations. The outcome of causal factors depends on interaction-patterns among them, and the way these change the structure of the system, and its operation, over time. Realistic analysis in this area poses a substantial intellectual challenge, and requires a departure from some long-dominant patterns of thought and language-use.

standards-lowering competition caused by international trade

Any workable society or group must have rules or norms that prevent its members from taking actions that would destroy the group. The pro football player, acting in his own interests, might make a tidy sum by selling the team's playbook to an opposing team—but that is not permitted. An American Army officer could increase his income by selling what he knows to certain other countries—but that would not be looked on kindly by the Army. A purchasing agent for a firm could augment his or her income nicely by taking bribes, an arrangement that would benefit both parties to the bribe—at the expense of the firm and its other members. Like other organizations, a nation works and survives because it sets standards of behavior, has rules limiting behavior that individuals might want to engage in but that would be excessively damaging to the society.

In economic affairs, many kinds of standards and rules are maintained by nations. The nations differ, however, in the kinds of standards and rules they define, and in the degree to which these are actually enforced. The great differences in the performances of the different nations depend importantly on these differences in their behavioral standards.

For such group-standards to be defined and enforced, however, the group itself must be well defined. It must have definite boundaries between itself and other groups, being separate or insulated from outsiders. The U. S. Army knows who is a member of its organization and who is not, as does the Chicago Bears organization, as does American Motors. Each organization makes its rules, distinguishes the members of the organization who are subject to the rules from outsiders who are not, enforces and lives by its rules, and succeeds or fails in part because of the wisdom and realism of the rules and standards it has made for itself.

Organizations necessarily take the position: "To enjoy the benefits of membership in this organization, you must follow the rules of the organization, which are designed to permit it to work and to survive." Would it not be anomalous for an organization to adopt the policy: "You may enjoy the benefits of membership in this organization by following the rules of this organization *or the rules of any other organization that you might prefer to substitute for them?*" Members of the organization then could shop around to find the rules that best suited their *personal* interests. Giving up the set of rules that defines its structure and determines the way it works, the organization would become a nonorganization, would not achieve its purposes and would fail.

These ideas apply to nations as well as to other organizations. To uphold civilized standards of life, achieve their particular goals, and work well enough to survive, nations make rules to govern economic dealings: The employer must protect the health and safety of his workers; firms must not sell foods or drugs that would damage the health of users, and so on. If such rules are to be enforced and to be effective, they must be applied equally to everyone, and an effort is made to do so.

But how do such national rules and standards work in international trade? In the case of unregulated trade across national boundaries, goods can be imported into the nation and sold there without meeting the standards and rules that the nation applies to goods produced at home (this is not true of "pure food and drugs" standards, but of most others). It is not asked whether goods imported from another country were produced under rules that protect the workers as thoroughly as they are required to be protected in the United States, were produced under the same standards of environmental protection that apply in the United States, and so on.

Unregulated international trade then creates an anomalous situation. The nation essentially says to firms: "If you produce within our borders, you must meet these standards and follow these rules, which have the effect of adding to your production costs. But you can evade all of these rules and standards, and avoid the costs they entail, by producing in some other country that has lax rules or no rules. And you still can bring the goods into this country and sell them in its market, just as if you had produced them here and met the same rules as local producers." In effect, the nation is saying: "You can evade the production standards and rules of the nation while retaining the benefits of selling in its market by shifting your production, and the jobs it involves, to another nation."

The effect of such an arrangement is to drive production and jobs out of nations that maintain high standards, to nations with few rules and low standards. Cost-cutting competition among firms forces this outcome, whether the owners and managers of the businesses like it or not. Under competition, it is not feasible to produce in a high-standards nation, because the lower-priced goods produced in low-standards nations will undersell you (unless, by chance, other factors offset this one). It is not reasonable to blame firms, or "capital," for this outcome. Competition forces it on them. The outcome can be changed only by altering the rules of the game.

The effect of maintaining high standards under conditions of free trade, thus, is to tell firms: "If you want to meet competition and stay in business, you must move production and jobs from our nation to some other place where low standards are permitted. You can take with you the capital that was developed in our economy, the expertise and production methods that were developed here, the managers that we trained here. Take them all abroad and provide jobs to people in a low-standards country and ship the goods back and sell them in our market—because to try to stay here and produce in our high-cost environment will only cause your firm to fail."

In a situation in which a number of nations are following such free-trade policies, the resulting interaction-process will cause nations to compete against one another in reducing standards and rules. Each nation will be under pressure to retain its jobs, its capital, its industries. Faced with firms that say, "If you do not remove this rule and the costs it imposes on us, we are going to have to shift production to Nation X, which has no such rule," the nation will decide that it no longer can afford to maintain high standards. Competition among nations will tend to force standards lower and lower.

This is an illustration of degenerative competition, or competition that causes socially damaging effects. Firms are forced to compete against one another in cutting costs by shifting production from high-standards to low-standards nations. This forces the nations, in an effort to retain or gain jobs and attractive industries, to compete against one another in cutting standards and abolishing rules.

An illustration of the operation of this kind of system is provided by the situation of state and local governments in the United States. Free trade prevails within the nation. States and localities can tax businesses and make rules to which they are subject. But competition among businesses forces them to seek the lowest-cost environment for their operations, to move away from localities whose rules involve high costs. This competition among businesses then leads to a competition among state and local governments to reduce their taxes and regulations, and even to subsidize businesses, in order to provide jobs for their people, and prevent the loss of tax base caused by the exodus of businesses from the locality. In recent years the competitive "war" among localities to attract businesses has led to tax concessions and local subsidies that made no sense at all from the nation's point of view.[10]

The structure of the system here in question involves competition at two levels, competition among businesses to cut costs, and competition among governments to retain businesses and the jobs they provide. At each level, the resulting process depends on a set of "rules," or structure-setting factors. Among firms, one rule is that they must compete against one another in cost-cutting; low-cost firms survive, high-cost firms fail. But the focus here is on an additional rule that operates along with this one under conditions of unregulated international trade: "Goods produced in one locality or nation may be freely sold in another one." Taken together, these structure-setting elements generate a system in which firms that shift production and jobs to low-cost locations and low-cost sets of rules and regulations will survive; others will fail.

National governments necessarily are under pressure to find jobs and income-earning opportunities for their people. If the prevailing rules enforce this game on firms, they enforce on governments a structure in which a government maintaining high production standards loses its industries and its jobs, while the nation that reduces or eliminates such standards gains industries and jobs.

How might the rules, or the structuring of the process, be altered so as to end this competition among governments in lowering production standards? To make production standards and rules identical for all nations is not feasible; there is no agency to make or enforce such a rule. Even if there were, this probably would not be a reasonable approach to the problem. Different nations confront different circumstances, have different standards of living, different population situations, different values. The high production standards that might suit a high-income nation that emphasizes the protection of its aesthetic values and its future generations might be quite unsuited to, and unenforceable in, an overpopulated, low-income nation with large unemployment that is having great difficulty meeting its month-to-month problems.

The approach to the problem that is feasible, and potentially reasonable, is to impose rules on international trade that put some sufficient limit on the importation of goods from low-standards nations into high-standards nations. What is required is not the prohibition of importation of goods from low-standards nations into high-standards nations. To impose such a rule would severely limit international trade, for in most cases of potential trade one of the nations will have production standards higher than the other, in one respect or another.

What is required is only to provide that the over-all package of trade is in balance, and in balance on terms that do not damage either nation. In this case, the specific thing that is to be accomplished by the trade-balancing mechanism is to remove the possibility for the one-sided shifting of production from high-standards nations to low-standards nations, with the goods being shipped to the high-standards nation to be sold.

If the trade is required to be in balance, this will not be possible. When it is not possible, the standards-lowering competition among firms is substantially eliminated. Removing the standards-lowering competition among firms has the effect of removing the standards-lowering competition among national governments, since they no longer have to compete against one another at lowering standards in an effort to hold or gain firms, production, and jobs.

What are some of the kinds of production standards and rules that are subject to degenerative competition among firms and among national governments under unregulated international trade? A partial listing may be helpful.

> Worker protection from on-the-job hazards, and provision of compensation for injury or death.
>
> Environmental protection of all kinds.

Preservation of natural resources, where this calls for methods of extraction that add to current costs, as in methods of harvesting timber and exploiting oil fields.

Pension systems, holidays, and "fringe benefits" of employment.

Limitations on child labor and the conditions under which women can work.

Restrictions on the length of the work-week and provision for overtime pay.

Unemployment compensation programs financed by taxes on firms.

More broadly, rules that exempt production from a production-related social cost—thus imposing the cost rather on workers, on future generations, or on other people.

In a world in which nations comprising a large part of the world's population are under enormous pressure to provide jobs for their people by whatever means they can, there exists great pressure for standards-lowering competition caused by international trade. The United States and other Western nations have in recent decades emphasized the raising of such kinds of economic standards. There has been little recognition that international trade threatens to undercut these standards and force them down to a very low level.

It will be seen, now, that to maintain national "standards" in these regards poses the same kind of problems as maintaining a high "standard of living" and high wage rates. From a human point of view, or in relation to the achievement of civilized patterns of human life, the raising of such standards may seem to be what economics, and economies, are all about.

But when the matter is viewed in relation to cost-cutting competition in "the free market," all of these standards are nothing but *cost-raising factors*. From a narrow, dollars-and-cents perspective, they are all sources of "inefficiency." They raise production costs! If one excludes human values, it commonly will be much cheaper to let a few workers be killed on the job than to install expensive safety equipment, surely so if no compensation need be paid for their deaths. And the "efficient" way to produce textiles or television sets is to use workers who work a very long day, and need to be paid only a pittance, enough for food, clothing, and shelter to keep them alive. It is this kind of "efficiency" that is enforced on firms—except where there are rules that make some more civilized and humane version of "efficiency" applicable.

But such rules to set high production standards cannot be applied on a nation-by-nation basis in a situation in which goods produced in one nation can be shipped freely into another nation and sold there. Under these conditions, competition among firms will cause production to shift to low-standards nations. Thus the nation that tries to maintain high standards will not only find that it finally must give up on them, but in the meantime will have lost its industries and its jobs to low-standards nations—a case, one might say, of adding injury to injury. This situation will impose on nations, in effect, a competition in lowering standards, causing a process of general regression toward economic barbarism.

This outcome, it must be noted, does not depend on there being any "villains" or "bad guys" in the story. The unhappy results arise from the way the game has been set up, from the rules that have been applied, rather than from anyone's violation of the rules. It would be foolish to point a finger of guilt at the undercutting of standards by those nations that have large numbers of people at the margin of starvation and can devise no other way to provide them with jobs.

The only hopeful approach, then, is to devise arrangements for international trade that prevent it from operating as a mechanism that drags production standards throughout the world ever lower. In this area as in others, what is wanted is a structure that generates cases of national economic success in achieving viable and civilized economic life—which then will set a pattern that can be copied and will finally bring success to other nations. What is most to be avoided is a structuring of human affairs that operates to make successes impossible, and drags all down to a low level.

instability and waste from international economic integration

Shifts in international trade and the international location of industries can be an important source of economic waste and instability. Differences in the situations of nations, inconsistencies in their policies, and abrupt changes in national policies pose a challenge to orderly economic arrangements. Firms contending against one another under competitive pressures commonly overreact to developments, as each tries to get ahead of, or at least keep up with, the others. The outcome is nonfunctional and damaging instability in exchange rates and in flows of funds between nations.

The rational and efficient arrangement of the location of industries in different nations poses, at best, a great challenge, given that the nations differ in their policies and in many other factors, and that many events have a future significance that is uncertain. But myopic private firms trying to avoid being left behind by others have been shown not to provide an effective instrument for dealing with this kind of decision problem. Abortive and stop-and-go shifts of firms and production between countries are to be expected under this arrangement.

Another source of instability and economic waste is "dumping." This is a practice of preserving a stable price and market conditions for a product in the home market by "dumping" a variable amount of surplus output into foreign markets, at whatever price the goods will bring, and thus inflicting on foreign countries the instability in market conditions and production that is being avoided in the home country.

And a conspicuously troublesome development for decades past, seemingly worsening since the rise of multinational corporations and other giant firms that can shift huge volumes of funds among nations, is "hot money movements." These are temporary shifts of funds from one country to another in pursuit of higher interest rates or of profits from changes in exchange rate. These temporary flows of funds affect interest rates and credit flows in the nations involved as well as exchange rates. Inappropriate behavior of interest rates and exchange rates can disrupt production and employment in the nations involved.

For example, say a hot-money movement into Switzerland raises the cost of Swiss francs to foreigners. This damages Swiss exports and the Swiss tourist industry, sending tourists to Spain where the exchange rate is more favorable. The losses of employment and output in Switzerland are a *real* cost of the episode.

Hot-money movements also can contribute to economic instability in the nations involved. The flow of funds from a nation with a recession and therefore low interest rates into a nation with a boom and therefore high interest rates will tend to worsen the departures from economic stability in both nations. The management of spending, output, and employment in a nation requires the national monetary authority to be able to treat the nation as a coherent money-flows unit, whose spending can be adjusted to its particular situation and needs. The pursuit by investors of maximum interest rates through the shifting of funds among nations tends to make each nation not a coherent economic unit. It brings about a kind of international economic integration that seems to serve no constructive purpose, and aggravates economic instability in the nations involved.

Thus a number of kinds of economic instability and waste can result from economic integration of nations, which pursue diverse and in some cases erratic economic policies, and which experience divergent changes in their economic conditions. An advantage would be conferred on a nation or nation-group that could avoid or limit these causes of waste and instability.

the imposition of insecurity or dependency on a nation by international trade

Another potential adverse effect of international trade is to impose on a nation a position of insecurity, vulnerability, or dependence on another nation. If a nation's economy comes to be built around materials imported from another nation, the cutting off of these imports could have disastrous effects. Dependency on a foreign market for the sale of the output of major industries—and thus for the means of financing the nation's essential imports—poses similar problems.

In such cases, the foreign government could use its ability to inflict serious damage on the vulnerable nation's economy to make extortionate economic demands, or to require political subservience. More commonly, action by the foreign government that is oriented to its own national interest, or perhaps that is simply erratic and irrational, can be a source of serious damage to a nation. Dependence on foreign sources for materials or goods required for the military defense of the nation poses a special problem that has conventionally been recognized by economics. But similar adverse effects on the self-sufficiency, and even the viability, of the nation can come from serious economic dependence on another nation.

At some times in the past it has been thought reasonable to assume that most nations could be induced to adopt and adhere to standards of consistency and responsibility in international relations and economic dealings that would minimize such potential problems. But recent developments show that this is an unrealistic expectation, at least for the foreseeable future.

The action of a group of Arab Oil Exporting Nations in collaborating to raise abruptly the export price of oil, and the initial tie of this action to an anti-Israel political position, illustrate that such a golden age of political amity and predictability has not arrived. A long list could be drawn up of actions and events in various nations that show how unrealistic it is to expect all nations to adhere to a code of exemplary conduct in international economic relations—or even to believe that they could agree on what kind of rules for national governments are desirable.

Thus, any actions that a nation can take—without violating standards of reasonableness or putting an unjustified burden on other nations—that reduce its vulnerability and its economic dependence on other nations merit serious consideration.

the undermining by international trade of the capabilities of the national government

Under free trade, governments are thrown into competition with other governments to attract and keep industries and jobs. They must compete by easing or abolishing laws and regulations that add to business costs. The necessity of doing this undercuts powers of government that are basic, and are needed for an effective national society. In giving a blanket permission for goods produced elsewhere to be imported into the nation and sold in its markets, the government is relinquishing the power to protect the nation's wage rates and standard of living against the depressing effects of overpopulation and low wage rates in other parts of the world. In another situation, the nation that has not achieved efficient organizations and production may find that even with low wage rates it cannot get any promising industries going in the face of competition from nations with tightly organized and very efficient production facilities.

One line of defense against the wage-reducing effects of overpopulation is the ability of the government to limit immigration of people seeking to escape the depressed living standards and lack of jobs in other nations. But this defense will be of little use if the same effects can result from the nation's jobs moving to low-wage labor in other nations. As was noted above, much the same effect results from the movement of industries and jobs from high-wage to low-wage nations as results from the movement of people from low-wage to high-wage nations. Both processes reduce wage rates in high-wage nations. They tend to equalize world wage rates at a level that reflects the influence of high birth rates and overpopulation anywhere in the world.

If the government cannot protect the nation's standard of living from being undercut by developments in other nations, it cannot protect the features of life that depend on a high standard of living: levels of education and medical care, housing, environmental protection, government services, welfare programs, support of science and the arts, the amenities of life, the achievements of civilization.

Moreover, if the government—as has been customary—gives individuals and firms the privilege of shifting funds into or out of the national currency without limit, it may thereby lose control over its domestic flow of credit and its interest rates. If people from other countries are free to shift their funds into the United States whenever United States interest rates are higher than those in other countries, the higher interest rates will not be sustainable—even though they serve the interests of the United States. In the opposite situation, low interest rates in the United States cannot prevail—even though they are what the United States economy requires—because people will shift their funds to other countries where interest rates are higher, and invest them there. The loss of coherency of the nation's savings-investment flow from excessive economic integration with other nations damages the government's ability to maintain prosperity and an efficient flow of new investment in the economy.

Competition with other governments to attract firms also affects the nation's ability to tax businesses in the way it deems appropriate. The government that loses its ability to impose desired taxes, regulations and standards for business activities, to control the nation's money supply, interest rates, and credit flows, to defend the nation's level of wage rates and its standard of living from the effects of overpopulation in other countries—what *is* this government capable of doing? Surely, it seems, not many of the things that need to be done in the present-day world to achieve an effective national economy and to sustain an advanced pattern of life.

This result is not at all surprising. Effective organizations, which can pursue their purposes and cause the outcomes they wish to cause, must have well-defined boundaries, and purposeful governance of activities within their boundaries. They cannot grant to outsiders the power to take actions that will thwart their purposes, destroy their governance, make them ineffective.

The conventional concept of "free trade" grants to individuals and firms privileges that are inconsistent with the ability of the nation to defend its economic interests, its standard of living, and its pattern of life. International economic integration necessarily nullifies the powers of individual nations, for integration merges them into a larger whole. But when the larger whole, the economically integrated world, is subject to no purposeful guidance, maintains no standards, but is propelled blindly forward, with no means of controlling or guiding the forces that have always had to be controlled or guided by civilized nations, the prospect is not an encouraging one.

International Economic Integration, Evolutionary Processes, and the Future

There are many different paths that human economic affairs could take in the decades ahead. Which evolutionary processes prove to govern events—from the enormous number that potentially could do so—depends on the way affairs are structured by national governments. For national governments are the only agencies in the present-day world that are capable of taking the required constructive actions, of applying knowledge and intelligence on behalf of the future achievement of human goals.

Preserving the effectiveness of the nation as an organizing and guiding unit of human life, avoiding a structuring of human relations that will cause a world-wide state of overpopulation-caused poverty, avoiding degenerative international competition among firms and among national governments that would force economic standards of many kinds downward—these are some essential goals for the decades ahead. The potential of unregulated international trade under the conditions of the present-day world to cause such catastrophic effects has not been widely recognized. A rapid awakening of understanding on this point, the speedy achievement of realism in the interpretation of international trade, may be critical for human prospects, and, in particular, for the future of the United States and the other precariously positioned nations of the West.

4

The Harmonious-Trade Area and International Trade

Economics has long distinguished between trade within a nation and trade across national boundaries, or "international trade." It has been claimed that these two kinds of trade work in basically different ways. Trade within a nation is said to be governed by "absolute advantage," or the absolute costs of goods, but international trade to depend not on absolute costs but only on "comparative advantage," or relative costs. This distinction was made as a basis for arguing that trade with a low-wage nation would not be damaging to a high-wage nation. We have seen that this distinction is invalid. International trade, like other trade, is governed by absolute costs. What is required to prevent a low-cost nation from generally underselling a high-cost nation is some mechanism that keeps the trade in balance.

To clarify this confused subject, it is necessary to raise the question: "What difference *does* it make if trade crosses a national boundary?" The conventional discussion is obviously muddled in that the properties said to apply uniquely to international trade are attributed to factors that apply to some cases of international trade but not to others, and that apply to some cases of trade within a nation: the distance involved, the transportation costs, the existence of cultural or political disharmonies, the legal and regulatory practices of governments. If these are really the governing factors, then whether trade is *international*, or crosses a national boundary, is of no importance in itself. If this is true, the assertion that international trade works in a basically different way than intranational trade must be false.

The continuing confusion on this point goes back, once again, to Adam Smith. In his treatment of international trade within the natural-harmony framework, Smith generalized from a particular example. He assumed that international trade was invariably trade over a long distance (which it is not), and that trade within a nation is always trade over a short distance (which *it* is not).[1] But the argument, then, applies not to *international trade*, but to *trade at a distance*. The argument would apply to early-1800s trade between eastern and western Russia, but not to trade between Belgium and northern France. And distance in general, we must recall, has lost the meaning it used to have.

Realistic interpretation of the effects of different types of international trade requires development of valid analytical categories, so that effects are attributed to the actual causal factors, rather than falsely attributed to factors that fit in with a set of ideological preconceptions. A basic intellectual benchmark needed as the starting point of causal interpretation of the effects of trade seems to be *the harmonious-trade area*. This is the hypothetical area within which trade has only beneficial effects, does not have destructive effects or lead to processes of degenerative competition.

After the concept of the harmonious-trade area has been defined and its significance clarified, it can be used as a point of reference in considering the kinds of policies or arrangements that are needed to avoid destructive effects of trade that crosses the boundary of a harmonious-trade area, or that is "external" to it. The goal is to define the kinds of arrangements that would be required in different kinds of cases actually to assure that the trade that occurs is beneficial to each of the nations involved.

The Concept of the Harmonious-Trade Area

The harmonious-trade area can be defined as an area within which there exist none of those inconsistencies or disharmonies that cause trade to have damaging effects. Trade within the harmonious-trade area would cause no degenerative competitive processes. The harmonious-trade area thus is an area over which trade requires no special regulations to prevent it from damaging a sub-area or nation. Thus, the characteristics that define the harmonious-trade area are the conditions that actually must be met for the conventional free-trade doctrine to be applicable.

To characterize the harmonious-trade area in a practical way requires considering the major kinds of damage potentially caused by trade and defining the conditions that must be met for these damages assuredly not to occur. The question then can be raised of what arrangements are required to avoid adverse effects in various cases of trade that is external to a harmonious-trade area.

situations analogous to the harmonious-trade area

The concept of the harmonious-trade area may at first seem strange, but similar ideas are taken for granted in many common situations. Consider the giving of examinations to students. Most students prefer that the examinations be honest, and social values call for them to be honest. But if there is an advantage in cheating, some students, following their own selfish interests in the matter, will cheat. To "let nature take its course," then, will result in cheating occurring, and the cheaters having an "unfair advantage" in examinations. This set of arrangements can create a situation in which only cheaters are successful. Examinations conducted in this way comprise a typical illustration of degenerative competition. Cheaters outcompete honest examination-takers; cheating behavior is subject to positive selection or positive reinforcement

To prevent this outcome, instructors customarily enforce on all a noncheating rule at examinations—a restriction on the "freedom" of the examination-takers. Enforcement of the rule and the actual prevention of cheating requires all students to "play by the same rules," and the rules maintained are those that support social values.

What is in question here can be viewed as the creation of a "harmonious-examination area," a situation in which the degenerative competition that otherwise would occur is prevented from occurring, and the required harmony is thus achieved. This requires the enforcement of a a common rule for all, and a rule that supports social goals—that has favorable general and indirect effects. To leave matters to "competition" in this case would lead to a *competition at cheating,* which would be undesirable. Since the giving of examinations customarily is approached on the basis of common sense rather than economic theory, it is usual to be aware of the issue expressed by the question, "Competition *at what?*" and to treat the matter in a reasonable way.

Another illustration of this class of case is competition between legitimate firms and firms run by criminal organizations. Again, the two play by different rules. The threats and violence applied by the Mafia organization give it an advantage. Firms that are unwilling or unable to compete at violence and extortion *fail* at the kind of competition that prevails, and go out of existence. The Mafia organizations take over. This is another characteristic illustration of degenerative competition. To avoid the degenerative competition and create a "harmonious-competition area" requires creating a set of *rules or laws* that prevent the damaging forms of competition, and enforcing these rules, so that firms are "all playing by the same rules," and the set of rules is one that is not damaging to the society.[2]

It is useful to note that in both of these cases the desired outcome does not occur "naturally." What is natural is for degenerative competition to occur, and the society to disintegrate. Success is achieved only through positive action on behalf of society, taken by government or supported by law. Nor is the accomplishment easy, simple, natural—or even fully achievable. Devising rules that will bring the desired results, and then effectively enforcing them, requires knowledge, judgment, organization, and discipline. What is accomplished is a human achievement, not a gift of Nature. These points need to be kept in mind because proponents of free trade and deregulation implicitly assume that any action of government that is difficult, or that cannot be perfectly accomplished, is thereby unnatural, and should be abandoned.

The harmonious area is not defined by a single dimension. Its requirements can include standards that have nothing to do with morality. In wrestling, for example, it is customary to structure competition in a distinctive way. A 130-pound wrestler who steps into the ring with a 230-pound wrestler is inviting an exchange that is unlikely to be mutually rewarding. Thus, a number of wrestler-weight categories are defined, and competition ordinarily is limited to wrestlers within a single weight-class. Why is this "unnatural restraint of competition" established? Because in open competition, the large wrestlers always would defeat the small ones, making the "sport" rather silly, and in this case brutal. The size categories can be thought of as creating "harmonious-wrestling areas" within which wrestlers can compete on roughly equal terms. Without this kind of rule, the sport could scarcely exist. This kind of segmentation, or creation of noncompeting groups, is common in sports—sports being an area that is mainly governed by realistic, experience-oriented thinking.

In such cases, insulated or noncompeting areas are established, through the purposeful devising of rules, to avoid a disharmonious situation in which one kind of person is generally defeated by another. A harmonious area in these cases requires that the competitors be about equally capable at the task in question, so that one does not always end up on the top of the heap, and the other on the bottom.

This case seems to have something in common with a much-discussed situation in international trade. When Alexander Hamilton asserted that the new and small American manufacturing enterprises could not stand up to the large and well established British firms,[3] he was saying the case involved such unequal competition, which would be severely damaging to America's prospects. Friedrich List later emphasized the same point about the industries of the belatedly uniting Germany.[4] Throwing the economies and the industries of many recently created African nations into competition with those of the West and Asia can be viewed as a similar case of unequal competition. It seems necessary to consider the possibility that such unequal competition in international trade is generally damaging to the weak competitor, so that a harmonious-trade area must include only sub-areas of equal competitive powers, or else must include some arrangement to assure that the unequal competition is not undesirably damaging to a sub-area.

It is a common idea that for any nation to decline to participate in free trade with any other nation is foolish, if not immoral. This notion was one factor behind the use of force by the United States, Britain, and other nations in the 19th century to require Japan and China to trade with them. But is that a reasonable position? Is it foolish or immoral for the 135-pound wrestler to decline to enter the ring with the 230-pound wrestler? Why does a nation have an obligation to engage in trade that will involve unequal competition or perverse competition that is potentially ruinous to it?

It is important to see that trade in the face of such a disharmony in competitive capabilities can be damaging to a nation even though it rests entirely on national differences in what can reasonably be called "economic efficiency." Suppose, hypothetically, that because of historical and long-standing cultural differences, Japanese and Chinese people do, and will continue to, work longer and harder than Westerners, to accept more stringent standards in quality of work, and to participate more dutifully and effectively in groups and organizations—doing this because it is their accustomed and preferred pattern of life. Would this difference between cultures cause a troublesome economic disharmony between the two areas?

If free movement of population were permitted in this kind of case, one people would tend to rise to the positions of superior power and wealth in both nations, coming to comprise the upper class of both societies. This is a situation that now exists in many nations, and that is a great source of conflict and political difficulties.

If migration were not permitted but unregulated trade prevailed, the less "efficient" society would finally have to accept a lower standard of living than the other one—even though the high-achieving society had a very low standard of living, say, because of overpopulation. Moreover, the society with the greater competitive power would tend to gain the rewarding industries, leaving the other society with the unwanted ones. This would put the societies on divergent evolutionary paths, which would widen their differences over time.

The less "efficient" society might be a quite viable economic unit, generating a way of life that its people found satisfying, if it were not forced into competition with societies that generally outcompete it. But forcing such a society into unequal competition could greatly worsen its position, and could make it no longer viable. These analogies between the harmonious-trade area and other types of harmonious and disharmonious relations between groups should be helpful in judging the conditions that must be met for international trade to be beneficial to the nations involved.

the requirement of desired oneness or wish to share

The harmonious-trade area, it seems, must be an area over which people want to "share and share alike," to become equalized, an area over which people do not distinguish "us" from "them," an area over which people wish wage rates and the standard of living to be equalized.

This condition must be met by the harmonious-trade area because competition operates to equalize prices and incomes over an area that permits unrestricted exchange and open access to markets. It is understood that the wage rate in Massachusetts cannot rise far above the wage rate for comparable workers in Louisiana when the Louisianans are free to move to Massachusetts to seek jobs, and when firms are free to move their production from Massachusetts to Louisiana in pursuit of lower labor costs, and then sell the output in Massachusetts. If the residents of the two areas do not wish thus to "eat from the same pot," they do not belong to a harmonious-trade area. Unrestricted trade between the areas will not serve their interests as they see them.

The harmonious-trade area also must be an area over which people do not care in what particular place the growing and promising industries are located—even though this will cause regional inequality of average incomes and opportunities. This condition is necessary because competition and specialization localize and concentrate certain economic activities. New York City is the recognized center for many business and artistic activities in the United States. A person who wishes to rise to the top in certain professions sees that this requires going to New York—it cannot be done in Boise or Beaver Dam. Because of the kinds of economic activities that are concentrated there, the average income may be much higher in such a city than in outlying areas.

Americans may be willing to accept a situation in which some professions can only be practiced at the top level in New York City. But they would not take kindly to a situation in which they could only be practiced in London, or in Tokyo. Americans might be unconcerned if some rewarding industries were to move from New York to California, but view the matter differently if the industries moved from New York to Taipei or Mexico City.

The existing nations do not necessarily comprise harmonious-trade areas. Indeed, the concept of the harmonious-trade area illuminates some serious conflicts that have occurred between regions and groups within nations over issues of trade. For example, the United States in the 19th century was torn between a South that desired a free-trade strategy suited to its becoming the world's specialized grower and exporter of cotton and a North that desired restrictions on imported manufactured goods to permit it to develop manufacturing industries in the face of the competition of British firms.

The Harmonious-Trade Area and International Trade 107

On the other hand, a harmonious-trade area conceivably could include two or more nations. The concept of the harmonious-trade area calls to attention the need to consider cases in relation to their paricular circumstances. Neither *international trade* or *intranational trade* is really homogeneous.

the harmonious-trade area and levels of wage rates

Unless people desire wage rates and incomes between two areas to be equalized—including people in the high-wage area whose incomes will be reduced— a harmonious-trade area requires wage rates and living standards that are approximately equal.

The relevant wage rates in such comparisons are efficiency-adjusted wage rates. For example, if southern wages are one-third lower than northern wage rates but southern workers accomplish one-third less per day than northern workers, then labor cost per unit of output is equal in the two areas, and the condition of harmony is met. Economic integration of the areas will not tend to reduce the wages of the northern workers. However, in this case the issue arises of the fragility of the condition. If, say, the southern workers are less efficient only because they are not combined with effective management, and the arrival of some northern managers will quickly make them as productive as norther workers, then the condition of harmony is not met.

rates of population-growth and expected future wage rates

Another factor that prevents an area from being a harmonious-trade area is differences between sub-areas in rates of population growth. Take the case of areas that have, say, equal wage rates at the outset but engrained customs of different family sizes and birth rates. In this case, the high-birth-rate group will, in time, increase its numbers so as to reduce the common wage rate, and the standard of living, thus affecting the character and the prospects of the society.

The high-birth-rate group also will increase its numbers in relation to the other group, and will in time come to dominate the area or society, a shift of power that is not likely to be well received by the group being pushed down to minority status by the high birth rate of the other group. The experience of a number of nations illustrates the group-conflict and the damage done to the capabilities of a nation by this kind of disharmony. For a group to merge itself with another group that has a lastingly higher birth rate is something like signing its own death warrant.

the harmonious-trade area and economic "standards"

The harmonious-trade area also requires common standards with regard to worker protection, environmental protection, resource conservation, and other such matters. Also relevant are policies with reference to commercial practices, and maintenance of competition, or anti-trust policy. An area receiving considerable recent discussion is standards in the prevention of infringement of patents and copyrights, and the sale of goods under false brands or labels. Equality in such standards is needed to avoid the shift of industries and jobs from the high-standards area to the low-standards area, and the imposition of degenerative, standards-lowering competition among the sub-areas of what then would be a "disharmonious-trade area."

uniformity of social goals and values

A further requirement of the harmonious-trade area is uniformity of all goals or values over the sub-areas and groups involved. The group placing a high value on preservation of the future quality of life will impose restrictions on present production and resource-use that will raise present production costs. These standards then will cause its production to be undercut by groups or societies that are oriented only to the present and thus impose no such restrictions, leading to a disharmonious situation.

Similarly, restrictions relating to aesthetic or other social values ordinarily add to production costs. The imposition of rules or standards by one sub-area to achieve these values could cause its production to be undercut by that of the area that did not enforce them. An extreme illustration of this type of factor is the disharmony in the pre-Civil-War United States caused by acceptance of slavery in the South and its rejection in the North, and the resulting fear of northerners of being forced into competition with the slave labor of the South.

Some kinds of high social standards may make for effective production and confer competitive advantages. Honesty, sense of responsibility, and a work ethic may be viewed as social values that can have an enormous effect, in direct and indirect ways, in making a society effective and thus making it successful in international competition. But it may be possible to maintain these values and standards only by geographic and cultural separation. The intermixture of high-standards people and low-standards people may result in the erosion of the high standards. In that case, the integration would be damaging to the area with the high goals and values.

On the other hand, a "work ethic" that brings economic success to a group is not necessary to be interpreted positively. A sub-group that favored a more relaxed way of life, or more emphasis on aesthetic experience and less on goods and money, might find itself greatly damaged by integration with an area of materialistic "eager beavers." Persisting in its preferred ways could cause the easy-going group to be reduced to second-class status in a society that came to be dominated by the hard-driving group. Many examples of this kind of disharmony are to be found, between nations and within nations.

Some of the potential disharmonies between areas or groups associated with differences in social goals and values would have their effects, or their full effects, only through the free movement of peoples; others would be effectuated by the movement of goods. The 1983 campaign of China against "cultural pollution" from the individualistic, hedonistic, and materialistic West illustrates that trade and related dealings may have some of the effects that would be fully felt only through the movement of people. Differences in social goals and values among sub-areas thus in various ways can prevent them from comprising a harmonious-trade area.

the economic theory and strategy underlying economic policies

Finally, differences in basic economic theory or economic strategy might prevent areas or nations from comprising a harmonious-trade area. An area preferring considerable regulation of industry probably would find its regulated industries undercut by the unregulated industries of a *laissez faire* area. The area or nation that preferred to rely on costs and prices to guide production and the nation that wished to use taxes and subsidies to adjust relative prices would find their economies in conflict.

A society enforcing competition by breaking up its large firms might find its atomized firms at a disadvantage in dealing with the large firms of another country. The nation choosing unregulated and price-governed international trade would find itself at a disadvantage in relation to the nation that managed its international trade to gain for itself the industries that would confer future benefits.

why the whole world cannot be a single harmonious-trade area

The doctrine of free trade treats the whole world as if it were without question a single harmonious-trade area. But when the issue is explicitly raised, it is clear that this could not possibly be the case. The various nations of the world do not face the same circumstances. They do not seek the same goals, nor apply similar policies. They do not maintain the same standards in economic activities.

And the differences among nations are not disappearing. The nations of the world are not moving toward economic and political all-alikeness. In the 1960s, it was widely believed that pre-programmed "economic growth" was going to make all nations alike—and all like the United States. But the experience of the past twenty years should by now have laid that notion to rest.

The nations have changed in diverse directions, growing in some respects more unlike one another in recent decades.

France, Iran, China, Argentina, India, Nicaragua, Hungary, the Soviet Union, Japan, the United States—obviously they are not becoming alike in the ways that would be required to make them a harmonious-trade area.

It is reasonable to expect that nations, existing with different backgrounds, in different circumstances, and acting out divergent ideological scripts, will continue to behave differently, pursue different economic policies, and follow different evolutionary paths. "One world," therefore, a homogeneous, all-alike, world of undiffentiated human beings living in undifferentated nations does not exist, and is not going to exist. Homegeneity, all-alikeness, is not the way of living things. Their evolution derived from their diversity, and they will continue to generate diversity. Successful arrangements for international economic relations must be oriented toward this kind of world.

"The principle of comparative advantage" of the orthodox economics seems to assert that *international trade* is basically different from other trade in that it does not need to be harmonious. *International* trade is depicted as involving a special corrective mechanism that nullifies the adverse effects that otherwise would result from such disharmonies as divergent levels of wage rates. This conception proves, on consideration, to be false. There is nothing about the passage of trade across a national boundary that sterilizes it, frees it from the damaging effects it otherwise would have.

The concept of the harmonious-trade area is thus a useful tool for defining the kinds of arrangements that will be needed to protect the interests of humanity's diverse societies, avoiding the destructive effects that otherwise can result from trade that is not limited to harmonious-trade areas, and permitting mutually rewarding trade between nations to be arranged even under these conditions.

The Harmonious-Trade Area and General "Externalities"

The concept of the harmonious-trade area relates in an interesting and illuminating way to that of "externalities," or effects that fall upon people other than those that decide on the actions. In the hypothetical world of economic theory, under ideal conditions, self-seeking actions by people and firms lead to the best possible equilibrium position. But economists agree that this happy outcome occurs only when the effects of actions fall only on those who determine the actions, that is, in cases involving no significant externalities. The orthodox economics treats this no-externalities case as the typical and important one. Critics of the orthodox economics argue that this is unrealistic. Externalities, they say, are ubiquitous, and will ruin the performance of an economy if arrangements are not provided to prevent this.

An illustrative case of an externality is a deal between A and B that is not socially defensible because it damages C, who was not a party to the deal. Since C does not get a "vote" on the decision, the damage done to him or her is ignored in the decision. Valid decisions should be made in the light of *all* of their significant effects. Thus, decisions that disregard some effects are not justifiable. An action can be justified only if it benefits all of the people affected, or in some workable sense brings a net benefit to all of those who are affected.

In relation to these ideas, dealings within the harmonious-trade area are not subject to certain kinds of systematic externalities that apply to whole categories of dealings. Unregulated trade over an area that is not a harmonious-trade area will result in whole categories of transactions that damage people who did not get a voice in determining the actions.

Permitting unregulated trade between a high-wage and a low-wage society, for example, presents a general incentive for mutually profitable deals between workers in the low-wage society and firms in the high-wage society, deals that are damaging to workers in the high-wage country—and indirectly to others. The employers will save labor costs by shifting their production to the low-wage society. The workers of the low-wage society will escape unemployment or get some increase in pay by taking these jobs. Both of these parties to the deal benefit, at least in terms of the direct effects of the action. But damage is done to the workers in the high-wage society. They lose their jobs, but are not participants in the transaction that determined their fate. Also to be regarded as externalities are the indirect damages done to the high-wage society from the decline in its standard of living. The shift of industries and jobs affects all of the people of the society, and future generations as well, but the governing decisions are made by a small number of people, who necessarily are pursuing their personal interests. Individualistic decisions systematically damage the interests of the society.

Recognizing the role in economic affairs of complex evolutionary processes brings out how ubiquitous are economic externalities. Very few economic actions affect only the parties that determine the actions. Many kinds of international transactions have far-reaching chains of consequences. Their full effects may bear little relation to the limited goals of the firms and people determining the actions.

The various kinds of degenerative competitive processes that potentially result from unregulated international trade thus can be thought of as involving systematic externalities that apply to whole categories of transactions. Jobless people in a low-standards society are happy to take the new jobs offered by industries that have shifted from a high-standards society in order to save costs. Buyers in the high-standards nation buy the imported goods because they are cheaper, and each buyer assumes that his or her action has no significant effect on the welfare of the nation. The firms are moved to the action by the cost-saving—or forced to it by inter-firm competition at cost-cutting. The interests of the people in the high-standards society who lose their jobs, and of the people of the society who are damaged by the shift of industries from the nation or the reductions in standards that are made to combat it—these all can be thought of as externalities. The people damaged did not get an effective vote on the actions that damaged them.

Interests that critically affect the future success or failure of the society are not represented in individualistic dealings in this kind of case. To avoid such massive and destructive externalities requires, it seems, avoiding the economic integration of areas that do not comprise harmonious-trade areas. This does not require avoiding all trade across the boundaries of harmonious-trade areas. But it does require that the trade reflect something more than the private interests of the traders. It requires some framework or procedure that represents the interests of the nations, and in doing so prevents general economic integration of the disharmonious areas.

arranging international trade as trade between the nations

The foundation of the mutualistic economy is the proposition that—within limits—individuals and firms are the best judges of their own interests, and are to be left to define and serve their interests as they see fit. They do this through voluntary dealings with one another. Each firm or individual enters into deals thought to be advantageous to it, and declines prospective deals thought to be harmful.

This arrangement is workable only within a set of rules and moral standards that prevents, say, A and B from striking a deal from which they both benefit at the expense of C, or at the expense of the nation. That is, constructive dealings must occur within a framework that limits harmful externalities and degenerative competitive processes. For people, groups, firms to pursue their own interests without a constructive framework of laws or rules, in a state of anarchy, does not work well. Too many people and organizations take actions that benefit themselves at the expense of others, and the degeneration of the situation into "a war of each against all," in Hobbes' phrase, reduces mankind to a degraded state.

How is this familiar way of interpreting economic affairs to be applied to the case of international trade between nations that do not comprise a harmonious-trade area? The nation is the dominant unit over which economic success or failure occurs: England makes an economic rise until the 1900s; Spain sinks into a prolonged decline when its gold-inflow ends; Japan rises and the United States falters. Such is the pattern of events.

Straightforwardly applying the logic of the mutualistic economy at this level of organization calls for trade across national boundaries, which so affects the success or failure of nations, to be arranged between the *nations*, between the national governments. Just as trade between Campbell Soup Company and American Can Company is conducted by officials of the two companies acting on behalf of the companies, so trade between England and Portugal would be conducted by officials of the English and Portuguese governments, acting on behalf of the governments, the nations, and the peoples of the two societies.

This arrangement would apply to this case the usual logic and protective features of voluntaristic trade. If American Can Company judged that a particular trade deal, a contract, would be damaging to the Company, the Company would say, "No." The trade would not take place. Similarly, if England, represented by its government, judged that an increase in imports from Portugal would damage England—say, by undercutting English wage rates and living standards—then England would decline that trade package.

Dealing with the problem of externalities generally requires an input from a higher organizational level, from a wider viewpoint, which permits "internalization of the externalities." Interests that are external to the firm and the individual are not ordinarily external to the nation, which is the organization applying the broadest view to economic choices. Thus, shifting the organizational level of decision-making upward from firms and individuals to national governments is the straightforward way of dealing with widespread and systematic externalities arising from international trade.

Moreover, trade arranged between nations potentially offers each nation protection against the various hazards of international trade discussed above. By permitting only trade deals or trade packages that are deemed advantageous to the nation, the government saves the nation from patterns of trade that would damage it.

A harmonious-trade area is defined to be "harmonious" in the sense that the self-serving actions of individuals and firms do not lead to major externalities and destructive processes. But trade that is external to a harmonious-trade area does involve this threatening potential. Thus, it is not reasonable in such cases to permit unregulated trade by firms and individuals. Mutually beneficial trade between the nations is not precluded, but such trade must be arranged by the governments, acting on behalf of the two nations.

The general logic, then, is that the individual makes decisions that advance and protect himself or herself; the family makes decisions that advance and protect itself; the firm makes decisions that advance and protect itself; and the nation makes decisions that advance and protect the nation—acting on behalf of its people. This can be viewed as the basic logic of a system in which individuals and organizations pursue their own interests within a framework that protects their common interest in the success of the society and the social system within which they live and work.

For the government to approach international trade in this way would be consistent with other aspects of its dealings with other governments. And the government acting in this way would confront the same kind of situation and the same kind of challenges that individuals and firms confront in making their decisions at their organizational levels. At none of these levels is there any simple formula that guarantees success. At each level, apart from accidents of fortune, success depends on knowledge, intelligence, organizational capabilities, realistic planning, foresight, and wisdom. Thus—as is equally true of people and of firms—the more competent governments will tend to score the better results.

In confronting its international-trade function, the government, like the firm, would seek to arrange coherent trade deals or trade packages that permit rational planning and evaluation. The contracts signed must fit into a pattern that accomplishes the purposes of the firm, or the nation. The contracts, and the over-all set of contracts, are to be evaluated in terms of their anticipated effects. Will this set of trade arrangements benefit the nation? Among the trade arrangements that could be arranged for the nation at this time, under the circumstances that exist, is this the best that can be done? These are the basic questions to be asked.

A point illuminated by the conception of the harmonious-trade area is the existence of a hierarchy of decision-levels. On some matters, the person decides for himself or herself. On others he or she defers to the interests of the family, or the firm, or the nation. The level at which decisions must be made depends on the case, and the potential that exists for external effects and damaging cumulative processes. Several kinds of differences between nations are the basis of economic disharmonies that require decisions to be made at the only level that can directly protect the interests of the nation, at the level of the national government.

what is accomplished by prearranged balance in international trade?

The national government arranging its international trade through contracts with foreign governments would naturally arrange for its trade to be in balance—or for the trade transactions plus approved capital transactions to be in balance. Handling this matter in an intelligent way would implicitly take care of most of the damaging processes and externalities that otherwise could result from unregulated trade crossing the boundary of a harmonious-trade area.

If the management of national trade policy is organized in a suitable way, those arranging trade on behalf of the nation would find their attention called to implications of the trade transactions that private traders would not care about or would have no basis for evaluating. The private trader has no occasion to ask, "What are the implications of this trade deal for the deficit or surplus in the over-all trade balance of the nation?" Or to ask, "What damage will be done by this deficit in the nation's trade and the implied shift of jobs to other nations?" Or, "What industries will our nation lose or gain as a consequence of this pattern of trade, and what effect will that have on the nation in the decades ahead?" But the management of a nation's trade policy can be structured so that those who arrange trade on behalf of the nation have a clear responsibility to confront these questions. If they confront them and deal effectively with them, they will protect the nation against the damaging effects that its international trade otherwise could have.

It is characteristic of trade within a harmonious-trade area that it does not raise the major questions and problems here considered. It meets the special conditions that must be met for unregulated private dealings to be compatible with the public interest.

prearranged balance in trade, and the threat of external low-wage competition

How does prearranged balance in international trade cope with the potential problem that a high-wage area will find its standard of living undercut by trade with a low-wage area outside of the harmonious-trade area. This would be caused by a one-sided movement of industries and jobs to the low-wage area, leaving the high-wage area with unemployed people and a balance-of-payments deficit.

What forces the high-wage area to accept reductions in wage rates and living standard is its high level of unemployment and the deficit in its international payments. The high-wage area confronting this plight can achieve balanced trade with the low-wage nation and make jobs for its people only by accepting equalization of the wage rates in the two nations and reductions in its own wages (in the absence of some inherent advantage of the high-wage area). Within the harmonious-trade area, this problem would not arise, either because the wage levels were already equal or because the equalization caused by the trade would be aggreable even to those whose incomes would be reduced.

But if the governments of the two areas prearrange a trade package that involves balanced trade, the problem does not arise. Under this condition, the high-wage area does not confront a deficit in this external trade. The value of the goods flowing into the area is not greater than the value of those flowing out. This implies that there is no net movement of industries and jobs from the high-wage area to the low-wage area. An independent constraint is imposed on the ability of firms to ship goods produced abroad into the high-wage nation. Thus, no general increase in international-trade-caused unemployment will occur in the high-wage nation.

Enforcing the condition that trade between areas be balanced suffices to avoid wage-integration between the nations. It actually brings about the condition that is assumed in the examples that are offered in erroneous justifications of free trade. It thus avoids the potentially enormous consequences of world wage rates being pulled downward to a lowest-common-denominator level that is set by the world's overpopulated, low-wage nations. So it was not unreasonable, as Adam Smith said it was, for pre-Smithian writers to argue that the government should concern itself with balance in international trade in order to protect the nation against potentially severe damage. Nor is it unreasonable today for a nation to be concerned over the implications of trade with efficient low-wage nations.

prearranged balance in trade and the threat of being undersold by a technically advanced nation

Consider also the opposite kind of case in which the superior efficiency, organization, and experience of a technically advanced nation cause it to under-sell a low-income nation that has lower wage rates than it does. A factor in this situation is that the "advanced" nation can produce products that the low-income nation is incapable of producing. In this case, other factors more than overbalance the differential in wage rates, so that it is the low-income nation that faces an intractable deficit in its international trade, the exporting of jobs, and pressure for further reduction in its wage rates and standard of living.

Once again, the prearrangement of balanced trade protects the interests of the area that is threatened by the trade outside the harmonious-trade area. It protects the less-developed nation against the debilitating inflow of products from technically advanced nations, accompanied by a deficit in international payments or deterioration in exchange rates and living standards. The balance in the trade package prevents the technically advanced nation from underselling the other nation and flooding it with products for which it lacks the means to pay.

prearranged balance in trade, and standards-lowering competition

Similarly, the prearrangement by governments of balance in trade limits or prevents standards-lowing competition. The high-standards area is not faced with the problem of a net shift of industries to the low-standards area. The limitation on the quantity of goods produced in the low-standards nation that can be shipped back to the market of the high-standards nation removes the incentive for firms to shift production to the low-standards nation. A low-standards nation potentially has some ability to use its cost-advantage to gain the industries that it deems rewarding. But as is pointed out below, it will be able to do this only if the high-standards nation acquiesces in its choice of the goods it is to export.

Once again, it is clear that the disharmony of economic conditions between the areas is not a matter that can be handled constructively by the self-seeking decisions of private traders. The scope of their interests, their goals, their knowledge, and their responsibility is not sufficient to achieve a pattern of balanced trade that will protect the nations. Thus, such decisions can be made validly only at a higher organizational level, at the level of the nation.

prearranged balance in trade and the location of attractive and unattractive industries

What of the hazard that trade across the boundary of the harmonious-trade area will cause the promising industries to shift elsewhere, leaving the area specializing in lines of production that have no future? The prearrangement by representatives of the nations of a package of balanced trade necessarily raises the issue of which products are to be exported and imported by each area, and thus of the national location of industries. The government that arranges for its area to import the goods of the attractive industries and export those of the unattractive industries is putting its area on the road to second-class economic performance, or failure.

There is no automatic mechanism to which this matter can be consigned. Which industries will prove rewarding in the future must be estimated on the basis of knowledge, analysis, and judgment. The particular capabilities of an area and the social values it wishes to emphasize also properly enter into the decision. The economic fate of an area, then, depends on the realism and foresight of its government in identifying lines of production that will be rewarding to the nation, and its competence at arranging trade deals that will make the best possible use of the capabilities and resources of its nation.

The Harmonious Monetary Area

The significance of the harmonious-trade area may be further illustrated by considering the related concept of the harmonious monetary area. Here, the question is what area would be best served by using the same money. A related question is how monetary relations should be handled for nations using different moneys. International trade cannot be properly interpreted without some knowledge of this subject, for the kinds of processes that are set in motion by imbalance in international trade depend on the existing monetary arrangement.

Two nations might agree to use the same money or to use separate national moneys. If they use separate moneys, the governments might keep their values linked together. The nation's monetary arrangement is important in two major connections.

First, its monetary arrangement affects the nation's ability to adjust the rate of spending for its output to its requirements, and thus its ability to maintain prosperity and economic stability. With modern monetary systems, the quantity of money in a nation ordinarily is continually changing. When new money is being created and injected into the nation's flow of spending and incomes, this tends to increase spending and to push the nation toward prosperity—or, in excess, into inflation. In the opposite case, when the quantity of money is declining, money is being pulled from the nation's flow of spending and incomes. This tends to make for a recession or a condition of economic slack. But if changes in the quantity of money are managed so they just suit the requirements of the economy, they can contribute to keeping the nation's spending on-target. This is what is required to maintain economic stability and prosperity. For the nation to have an independent monetary arrangement gives it the power to manage the quantity of its money unusually well and enjoy the benefits of the resulting prosperity and economic stability. But, of course, a nation can use its power over the quantity of its money badly, and suffer the burdens of the resulting instability, inflation, or depression.

In this connection, the harmonious monetary area is an area with common monetary requirements. The major defining characteristic is the behavior of wages, costs, and prices in the area. Within an area that shares the same money, if Region A has laws and institutions that bring stable costs and prices while Region B characteristically generates an upward push of money wages, costs, and prices, then Region B will find itself undersold by Region A. It will find that the flow of spending of money is not large enough to take its full-employment output off the market at its rising level of prices. When Region A has prosperity, Region B will have economic slack or depression. The two areas thus do not comprise a harmonious monetary area. They generate behaviors of costs and prices that are disharmonious. They can perform better with separate moneys, so each can adapt the quantity of its money to the flow of spending it needs to maintain prosperity.

The second broad implication of the national monetary arrangement is its effect on what happens when international payments are not balanced. The "adjustment mechanism" that goes into operation when a nation has a deficit, say, in its international payments determines the particular kinds of burdens and problems it confronts as a result of being undersold by foreign producers.

If two nations use the same money, or are monetarily integrated, and one of them is underselling the other because of its lower wage rates, the shift of industry and jobs from the high-wage to the low-wage area works out directly through ordinary transactions. The firms in the high-wage nation cannot sell their products. They lay off workers and cut back production, while the opposite changes are occurring in the low-wage nation. The

The Harmonious-Trade Area and International Trade

high-wage nation finds itself in a continuing economic depression; the low-wage nation enjoys prosperity. The "adjustment mechanism" that would end this unequal situation is the equalization of wage rates in the two nations, and the acceptance by the high-wage nation of the reductions in wage rates that are required to permit its workers to compete on equal terms with the workers of the low-wage nation.

If the nations have different moneys, imbalance in their trade and payments will tend to affect the exchange rate between the two moneys, though what happens in such a case depends on the exchange-rate policies of the nations. With flexible or cleanly floating exchange rates, there is a reduction in the international value of the money of the high-wage nation with a deficit in its international payments. The decline in its exchange rate and the foreign value of its money is another way in which it can cut the prices of its goods to foreigners. If the international value of the dollar declines, for example, American goods become cheaper in terms of foreign currencies, and foreign goods become more costly in the United States. Thus, such a change in exchange rates is an alternative way for a high-wage nation to cut the prices of its goods to foreigners in order to meet foreign competition. In doing this, it is implicitly reducing its wage rates and its standard of living.

The change in exchange rates increases the cost of imported goods and "the cost of living." By accepting the resulting decline in the purchasing power of their incomes, people accept the reduction in their real wages and incomes to meet the foreign competition. If the people refuse to do this, and demand increases in their wage rates and incomes to offset the increase in prices, then the adjustment does not occur. Then the nation experiences continued economic slack, inflation because of the upward push of wages and incomes, and continued decline in its exchange rate because of the inflation. Other monetary arrangements such as pegged exchange rates, exchange rates with an adjustable peg, or managed exchange rates involve different combinations of these ingredients.

Perhaps, three points relating to harmonious monetary areas are worth keeping in mind. First, the design of monetary arrangements, like the design of arrangements for international trade, should focus on the relations between the economies involved, the extent and character of the disharmonies between them. There is no one arrangement that will suit all cases, no "natural" arrangement. Human design, foresight, and knowedge are the basis of success.

Second, changes in exchange rates (in the relative values of the moneys of the nations) may be a part of the process that results from unbalanced trade between nations. But such changes in exchange rates do not provide an "adjustment mechanism" that prevents damage to the nations involved. Rather, they are a part of the process by which the damage to a nation occurs. To the nation that is being generally undersold in international trade, changes in exchange rates do not offer a means of escaping from the unhappy consequences of this position, but are a means by which the unhappy consequences are inflicted. In economics textbooks and articles, the impression is often conveyed that changes in exchange rates achieve needed "adjustments" without any nation being damaged—and this is how it is that "free trade" works so perfectly. This is the kind of error that can result from considering a subject at too high a level of abstraction, so that preconceptions dominate the interpretion. Evidence, experience, and the actual processes by which changes in economies occur are neglected. A consideration of the actual processes involved shows no way in which changes in exchange rates can permit a nation to escape the dire consequences that could result from being generally undersold in international trade and losing its industries and its jobs.

Third, it must be kept in mind that when a nation undergoes "adjustments" by experiencing economic slack or recession because of the loss of its industries, or experiencing inflation because of the decline in its exchange rate, these events change the position and the capabilities of the nation. They do not leave the powers and the behavior of the nation as they were. Continued depressed economic conditions cause business losses, the extinguishment of the nation's capital, the loss of firms through failure, the loss of people's skills from unemployment, the demoralization of people from prolonged unemployment, changes in attitudes and political beliefs—and these changes can decisively affect the performance of the nation at the next stage of the game of international economic competition. Similarly, inflation, once begun, can become habitual, self-feeding, difficult to limit, and impossible to expunge from the nation's experience. It has become conventional in economics to depict some "adjustment mechanisms" for international payments as if they painlessly made the desired "adjustments" and had no important side effects. Unfortunately, in some cases the unhappy side effects may be the most lasting and important effects of the episode.

Constructive International Trade Amid Economic Harmonies and Disharmonies

It is not the way of the world for relations among living things to be automatically mutually advantageous. Among plants and animals, one finds dealings that are mutually rewarding, others that are one-sided, parasitic, some that are mutually destructive. Evolutionary selection in this kind of world has provided many species with wonderfully elaborate strategies of self-defense against those who would victimize them.

Nor are self-protection or mutually advantageous relations brought about by applying some simple, universal, verbal principle. The world seems not to effectuate any simple formula or principle. Mutually rewarding relations are complex and diverse, fitting the circumstances of the particular cases. The relation between wolves and moose and that between bees and clover are both mutually beneficial, but are quite different relations involving different kinds of benefit. The pattern of relations among an organized local group of lions is diffrent from that of wolves, bees, gorillas.

It hardly need be said that the relations between individual human beings are not always mutually beneficial, and it does not seem that any simple, universal rule would make them mutually beneficial. Similarly, the actual relations between nations have been complex and diverse—and assuredly not always mutually beneficial.

How could it possibly be, then, that a simple rule like "free trade," which quite ignores the diverse circumstances and goals of nations, could cause them to have mutually beneficial economic relations? In the light of experience, and of the understanding of present-day science as to how the world works, it seems that such a thing cannot be. What is asserted is unnatural, supernatural. That is, indeed, what it is. The doctrine comes from the myth of the seventeenth and eighteenth centuries of a harmony under economic individualism that was magically preprogrammed by Nature.

To think about international trade within a modern, cause-and-effect framework calls for interpreting the effects of economic dealings across national boundaries in terms of the distinctive features of each case. The circumstances, behaviors, the goals of the nations fit together in ways that create potentials for both constructive and destructive processes, according as the positions of the nations are harmonious or disharmonious. Dealing with economic reality requires the analysis of these harmonies and disharmonies and the dynamic processes to which they can lead. Such analysis must underlie the design of a system of international trade that utilizes the available benefits from harmonious international trade, while avoiding the destructive effects that can come from individualistic trade across the boundaries of nations that are subject to serious economic disharmonies.

5

Patterns of International Trade

Some patterns of international trade that might develop over the decades ahead call for further consideration. The goal is to form a realistic picture of the patterns of events that actually would occur under different sets of rules and policies in the world as it now exists.

Kinds of National Policies toward International Trade

Economics textbooks, newspaper editorials, and policy discussions commonly present only two approaches to international trade, "free trade" or "protectionism." "Free trade" is depicted as The Good, the right thing to do, leading inevitably to the best-possible outcome. "Protectionism" is depicted as harmful, and supported by people only out of ignorance or narrow selfishness.

Policies toward international trade cannot be realistically interpreted in terms of these stereotypes. The available polices, and the policies that actually are practiced, are more numerous and more complex than this. A more accurate list of types of policy toward international trade, which will serve to open up the subject, might be given in this way:

(1) A policy of self-sufficiency, autarchy, or minimum economic involvement with other nations. For example, Japan and China tried to remain insulated from Western commerce in the nineteenth century. They proved to lack the power to do this, and suffered severe consequences.

(2) The strategic-developmental approach in which a nation tries to gain the industries that offer high rewards and are expected to lead to a cumulative process of national economic betterment. This was more the rule than the exception among those European nations capable of applying it until recently. It is exemplified recently by Japan, South Korea, Taiwan, Singapore, the nations providing the great economic success stories of recent decades.

This approach does not lead to a standard pattern of policy actions, because different nations confront different circumstances, set different targets for themselves, choose different developmental strategies, and form different judgments as to which industries will be the high-payoff ones.

(3) The use of political power, shrewdness, or superior skill to gain exceptionally favorable terms of trade with other nations, in a sense, to exploit their weaknesses. The Nazi government of Germany developed this approach to a fine art. Critics say the trade of the Soviet Union with its satellite nations sometimes includes such an element.

(4) Trade arranged directly between government agencies only. This is the typical form of trade of centrally planned economies.

(5) Trade of a colonial power with its colonies. This commonly was arranged by the colonial power on the basis of the view that certain advanced industries, primarily manufacturing, were especially rewarding. These were to be retained by the

colonial power. The colony was to play the complementary role of supplying raw materials and providing a protected market for the advanced products of the colonial power.

(6) Special economic integration within an area, or a trade bloc, such as the European Economic Community, with higher barriers to trade with outsiders. This is one pattern of international economic relations that distinguishes among nations in the degree of economic integration with them that is to be arranged.

(7) "Nondiscriminatory" trade in which the same restrictions on imports are applied to all foreign nations, as under the "most favored nations" approach. A tariff concession made to one nation is extended to all others.

(8) Thoroughgoing "free trade," with no restrictions on imports, in the extreme case no tariffs or quotas, trade being as "free" across national boundaries as it is within them. Though taken by individualistic economics as a theoretical ideal, this is an extremely rare case. Critics point out that this kind of policy is followed mainly by nations that gain a special advantage from being a trading center or nations that are in a position to have the upper hand in the trade, expanding their domination of the advanced industries by undercutting incipient industrial development in other countries. It often has been pointed out that this interpretation fits England's 19th-century propounding of free trade—after it had won its position of industrial dominance by playing a very different game.

(9) Bilateral trade agreements between the governments of nations. These have been in bad repute among those who thought of free trade as the desired goal. In part this reflects memories of the exploitive use of such agreements by the Nazi Government. But bilateral agreements such as that between the United States and Japan for a voluntary limitation of Japanese exports of automobiles to the United States have been used to deal with situations in which the results of unregulated trade were so damaging as to be unacceptable to a nation. When a realistic view is taken of the implications of unregulated trade, such agreements between governments will have to be viewed

in a new light, as a basic means of accomplishing balanced and mutually beneficial trade between nations.

Actual practice and experience with international trade thus is more complex and diverse than popular discussion of the subject would suggest. In considering the future development of international trade, it is important to interpret past experience in relation to these realities rather than misleading slogans and misstated either-or choices.

"Discrimination" in International Trade

To avoid an undesirable "discrimination," must the United States apply the same tariff rates and import restrictions to all nations? The recently dominant view says, "Yes." This view, and the "most favored nation" procedure for applying the same tariffs to all nations developed in the 1930s as a reaction against the undoubtedly undesirable brand of discriminatory trade policies developed by Nazi Germany.

Reacting against this exploitive discrimination in international trade, economists argued that the answer was to avoid all discrimination. A nation should apply to all foreign countries the same tariffs, as if they were all alike. A difficulty with that approach is that, in fact, foreign countries *are not alike* in the hazards they pose through unregulated trade.

If the United States and Germany comprised a harmonious-trade area, there would be no hazard to the United States in unregulated trade with Germany. But another country might pose a great hazard of loss of rewarding United States industries, for example, because this nation had low wage rates, low production standards, and a government that was effectively pushing for the take-over of these industries. In this kind of situation, is it reasonable to treat trade with Germany and trade with this other country as if they had the same effects—when, in fact, they have quite different effects?

The word "discrimination" often is used—if it might be so put—with insufficient discrimination. What is objectionable is not treating nations, or people, or ideas, as what they actually are, "discriminating" among them in a realistic sense. What is objectionable is treating people or nations differently when they are alike, or basing differential treatment on invalid or unfair criteria. Thus, it is unreasonable—and in a sense "discriminatory"—to treat nations as being alike when, in a relevant sense, they are different.

To treat A differently than B because he has hair of a different color is objectionable discrimination. But when considering them for a loan it would be reasonable to treat them differently if A has an exemplary credit record while B is a frequent defaulter; when considering them as members of a chorus it would be reasonable to admit B for his fine sense of pitch and exclude A for his tone deafness. The ordinary business of life becomes a shambles if people, organizations, and situations are not thus treated realistically, with relevant discrimination.

Following this line of thought, making a relevant differentiation of treatment among nations in international trade is not objectionable "discrimination," but only the kind of realistic response to situations that is required to achieve human purposes in a cause-and-effect world. For the United States to enter into close economic integration with West Germany, or France, or Canada, might be a reasonable action. For the United States to enter into close economic integration with a nation of the circumstances of China would be something close to insanity. Such is the reality to which reasonable policy needs to adapt.

Fairness and civilized standards of behavior call for treating different nations in a consistent way, in terms of policies that are not based on malice or efforts at exploitation of another nation. But the notion that all trading partners must be subject to the same tariffs, no matter how different are the consequences in the case of nations in different circumstances—this precludes a realistic approach to international economic relations and is a dangerous doctrine.

Another way of thinking about this point may be useful. It has been customary to hold that treating nations equally, or in a nondiscriminatory way, meant applying, say, the same tariff rates to each of them. Another conception of treating nations equally would involve applying to each of them policies that will cause trade between the nations to be in balance. We recall that balance in the trade between nations is necessary to protect a nation against potentially serious effects such as being generally undersold and losing its industries and its jobs. Thus it could be argued that for the United States to treat, say, England and Japan *in the same way* means arranging that trade with both of those nations should be in balance. But this criterion, of course, is quite in conflict with the criterion of applying the same tariff rates to the two countries. This line of thought also implies that the recently conventional ideas about nondiscriminatory trade are too narrowly conceived, and seriously unrealistic.

International Trade Is a Negative Influence

The view frequently is expressed that international trade and international economic integration, as such, are desirable. They make the world a better place. A continuing trend of increasing international trade and international economic integration also is often represented as inevitable, predetermined, and thus useless to complain of or resist.

These ideas need to be considered critically. Unless it is managed in just the right way, trade across national boundaries will be damaging to one or both nations. Unregulated trade across national boundaries opens an avenue for individuals and firms to evade the laws, rules, and standards of the nation. For them to do this sets up a standards-lowering competition that pulls others into the process. Actions that cut across the jurisdictions of national governments, and thus cannot be adequately dealt with by either government, tend to undercut the rules that prevent degeneration of economic life. Trade across national boundaries, thus, is not to be thought of as inherently desirable and beneficial, but as inherently threatening, requiring special arrangements to prevent it from being a damaging influence.

A number of kinds of damage that can result from the loss of social guidance of economic processes caused by unregulated international trade have been mentioned: the effective loss of control over population and the creation of an international process causing overpopulation-caused poverty; degenerative competition in lowering production standards; the general weakening of the powers and effectivness of governments. There is also the additional hazard of instability, and of the dependence of one nation on another. Such particular problems lie behind the generalization that the internationalization of economic activity to some degree removes it from effective human control, and makes man, and his civilization, his future the pawn of chance—or worse, dooms him to degenerative processes that guarantee a great fall.

Thus, realism requires adjusting to the idea that international trade is not a boon but a potentially hazardous activity. It can weaken and disorganize nations, and nations are home to human beings.

The Incommensurability of Potential Gains and Losses from International Trade

In some activities, the losses to be feared are commensurate with the gains that might be made. An investment in securities can lose no more than the sum invested, and promises a yield that is related to this invested sum.

But consider a case in which a person with a large fortune makes a small investment in a partnership. The possible gain is small. But because the partnership involves unlimited liability, if this business went badly the wealthy investor could lose his whole fortune. The possible loss in this case is out of all proportion to the possible gain. In the world of business, no reasonable person would put himself or herself in that kind of position.

Unregulated international trade is like the second case. It economically integrates the nation with other nations, and makes it subject to the consequences of actions over which it does not have control. Thus, again, the damage that might be done to a nation may be out of all proportion to its possible gain from the trade involved. Take a large, high-income nation like the United States, with little dependence on imports. What it can gain from unregulated international trade is limited. But what it can lose—is everything.

Unregulated international trade sets up a whole new structure of relations among nations, altering the prerogatives, powers, and performances of nations. A kind of trade of but limited possible benefit to the United States, thus, could basically change the economic position of the United States. From being an independent, reasonably self-controlled economic entity, it becomes an element in a larger, integrated economic entity. Its future goes out of its control. If the larger, integrated economic entity of which it has now become a part falls to a low wage rate and standard of living because of overpopulation, the United States winds up a failure—a failure to a degree that it would not likely have become had it remained independent.

Once again, this point merits emphasis because it runs against the beliefs that now are dominant in the United States. But one sees that it does not run against common sense, or experience. As does the wealthy person who joins a partnership and accepts the position of unlimited liability, the nation that accepts economic integration with other nations is signing a blank check—this is *unlimited liability*. In many cases, there is no conceivable gain from the arrangement that can offset the possible loss.

Potential Futures of a Troubled West: Struggling Upward, or a Great Crash

It would be idle to deny that the Western nations have in the past twenty years acquired a heavy load of self-imposed economic disabilities. Overloaded with expectations, commitments, excessive and conflicting demands of internal economic groups, costly government programs, habitual inflation, retirement and medical programs that cost too much, with citizenries more oriented to making demands than to great achievements, the Western nations, at best, seem to face a time of economic troubles. But if the West were not hit with blank-check burdens from international economic integration, one could imagine that some of the nations could work their way through this difficult period to something better, and that most would survive their disappointed expectations and make their required retrenchments in reasonable order.

But add to the picture the loss of major industries that had provided a significant part of their jobs and incomes, add intractable balance of payments deficits arising from importation of the goods they used to produce—add this to the rest of their picture, and how do the prospects look? If one considers the unfavorable case in which the industrialization of Asia and the deindustrialization of the West continues, what, then, would seem to lie ahead? If the West must absorb not only the results of its own past extravagances and unrealisms but also a great decline in wage rates and living standards and a continuing loss of jobs from the departure of major industries, how are these societies to be expected to react?

The potential for worsening group conflicts, irrationality, and extremism is obvious. For a nation to adjust efficiently to such a decline in hopes and expectations is rare. The West, already in an difficult economic position, could provide an all-time-great illustration that the costs to high-income nations of general economic integration with low-income nations can be out of all proportion to the possible gains.

The Location in Nations of Industries with Promising and Unpromising Futures

At any point in time, the different industries are not equally rewarding to the nations in which they are located. Some pay high incomes to the people employed in them, and a high rate of return to the invested funds. Others pay only low incomes, and low profits, or losses, to the firms involved. Some lead to cumulative processes of national economic advancement. Others lead to dead ends, prove to be sinkholes for the nation's capital, and its hopes.

factors that make an industry promising for the future

Which industries will be the most rewarding to a nation during a period of time? This depends on a number of interacting causal factors. Foretelling the future, in this as in other respects, is not easy, or riskless. But neither is it avoidable, to those who would cause their own success. Among the factors that make particular industries prospectively rewarding to nations that are involved in international trade and international industrial specialization are these:

(1) An industry is made promising by being in a rising phase, by prospectively growing in importance and size, with rising demand, rising output, and an increasing number of jobs.

(2) An industry is made rewarding by generating significant skills, know-how, practical knowledge that then will serve to keep the nation ahead of other nations, or to give it capabilities that they do not possess.

(3) For an industry potentially to be the basis of spin-offs of other new and rewarding activities contributes to its attractiveness. Such an industry can serve as a foundation from which the nation can in the future develop new and rewarding industries that cannot yet even be defined.

(4) Another kind of hidden or indirect benefit of an industry is that it develops in people and firms the kinds of knowledge, experience, and skills that will advance their capabilities at the kinds of tasks that will be rewarding in the future. For example, experience with large-scale manufacturing activities has provided the basic training in a range of activities that then proved to be essential for more advanced economic activities in many lines: in the design and management of large-scale rational organizations, in engineering and production engineering, in personnel management, financial management. The nation whose people and organizations had experience with such activities developed capabilities so far beyond those of the nation that remained in subsistence agriculture that from a production-capabilities point of view it is almost as if the two nations were peopled by different species.[1]

(5) It is a desirable feature of an industry that it is somehow protected from the intrusion of new competitors—and especially of competitors with any kind of cost advantage, such as that conferred by low wage rates. Such protection might be conferred by cutting-edge technology or technique that others

are unable to copy or to keep up with. Of course, in such matters expectations can be disappointed. Industrial espionage and the speedy copying of the achievements of others are among the booming "industries" of recent years.

In summary, perhaps it can be said that attractive industries are those that generate important or essential products for which others will pay high prices, that are in a rising phase, that develop the production capabilities of the nation, and that will not involve competition from efficient low-wage nations.

It is important to note that there is no theoretical or conceptual category of industries that is inherently rewarding. Technically advanced industries are not necessarily rewarding. The steel industry involves an impressive technology, but the widespread belief that steel was in some sense a "leading" or "key" industry led to the building of steel mills in many nations, to excess capacity, and depressed conditions in the industry. Thinking about industries in terms of theoretical or verbal groupings has not proved a valid way of identifying the rewarding industries of the future. Joining the rush into the fashionable industries has not worked well either.

what are the potentially rewarding industries of the present-day world?

Anticipating what industries will prove to be rewarding to the nation participating in international industrial specialization now must take account of the new and unique potential of today's international trade and international economic integration. This adds to the difficulties of a task that was in any case difficult enough.

That industries that are in a technical sense advanced—and that could not have been widely copied by low-wage nations in the past—now are not necessarily a good bet is illustrated by what happened to the steel industry, and to shipbuilding. The present-day transferability of techniques and the existence of a number of low-wage nations that are well organized and potentially very efficient producers has made industries that had been expected to be rewarding quite unrewarding—gravely disappointing the hopes of some nations.

The limited ability of firms and nations to protect their "trade secrets" in the present-day world could come to mean that the successful strategy is to let others bear the costs of innovation, and then quickly copy their discoveries, and undercut them on cost and price. The prevalent adoption of this approach, of course, tends to dry up innovations, to the ultimate detriment of all. Differences among nations in their ability to keep their trade secrets could come to be a significant determinant of which nations do best in the competition for rewarding industries.

An important determinant of which industries prove to be rewarding is the future change in the markets for those industries, which depends on the economic success or failure of different societies. In the recent past, a key to national success has been the gaining of industries that produce advanced goods, using new technology, for the markets of the high-income nations. But if the economic integration of the nations of the world continues, and if the income-equalization resulting from this economic integration initiates a process of reduction in wage rates and standards of living in what had been the high-income nations, then the kind of markets that have been the key to economic progress in the recent past will disappear. This will be a new kind of an economic world. In this changed world, the key to economic success—such success as is attainable by the nation that is dependent on international specialization and international trade—will have to be different than in the past. Looking ahead, the uncertainties are many.

The uncertainties and hazards of this situation present an unusual incentive to the nation that does not need to make itself dependent on international trade to limit its involvement in international economic intergration. Nations that are to some degree dependent on international trade and specialization have a strong incentive to manage their trade and specialization so that it is under some intelligent guidance, so that it is not the nation's ticket to an unknown and perhaps wretched destination.

The Potential Decline of the West from Economic Integration with Overpopulated, Low-Wage Areas

The potential effects of international economic integration are shown by a dismal scenario in which international trade operates to impose worldwide poverty caused by high birth rates and worsening overpopulation in some parts of the world. Exploring the process by which this unhappy outcome would be caused provides an exercise in analyzing the interconnections among nations that are imposed by international trade. It brings out that international trade and the developments it causes have the power to revolutionize the character of human life. In a practical sense, international trade can change human societies, and human beings, from what they now are to something very different.

the first stage of the process

Low-wage labor can be thrown into competition with high-wage labor by a change in circumstances or in the laws and policies of nations. Let us consider an illustrative case in which with rapid and cheap communications such as now exist and with low Western restrictions on imports, India and China undergo a shift in political leadership that puts their two billion people into effective production for Western markets. That is, assume that China and India seek to raise their living standards by using Western expertise and methods, whether within a capitalist or socialist framework, to produce for the large Western market—as have Japan, Taiwan, Hong Kong, South Korea, and Singapore. The international economic process that has been going on in recent decades would thus be pushed much further.

The effects of bringing a body of low-wage labor of equal producing capabilities into competition with high-wage labor by eliminating the barriers that earlier had prevented this competition is to cause production using the low-wage labor to displace production using the high-wage labor. Low-cost products undersell high-cost products.

In this case, labor is assumed to be prevented from moving from India and China to the United States. Thus, the adjustment is made by production moving from the United States to China and India. The shift could be carried out largely by United States firms. Each firm, realizing that if it continues to use high-wage labor it will be undersold and ruined by its competitors, must move its production in order to survive. Or expanded production in the new areas can come from foreign firms, multinational firms, or effective firms initiated by the Chinese and Indian governments, with United States firms declining and failing as their sales disappear.

This outcome depends on production being carried out efficiently in China and India. If production in these nations were so inefficient as fully to offset the advantage of their low labor costs, then they would not undersell Western production, and the chain of events explored below would not occur. Many factors can make production inefficient in a nation, political turmoil, lack of worker skill or discipline, prevalent graft, damaging government policies, and many other factors mentioned earlier. But, of course, these factors could be operating in Western nations more than in China and India, tipping the scales in the other direction. We here consider the case in which efficient production is achieved in the low-wage areas.

The effect of the economic integration through trade of the low-wage and the high-wage labor, then, is to shift industry and jobs from the high-wage to the low-wage nations. As an illustration, the United States finds industries and jobs leaving the country. Goods that used to be produced here now are produced in the low-wage country, and imported from it. Western workers lose their jobs in the declining industries, and do not find expanding industries that are offering comparable jobs to which they can shift.

The Western nations also find themselves with a deficit in their international trade. The shift of industries has reduced their exports and increased their imports. Ordinarily this would lead to a deficit in their international payments. The typical Western nation is buying from abroad more than it is earning with its exports. The low-wage foreign production undersells its products not only in its home market but also in foreign markets to which it used to export—as was the case for the North Italian textile industry when it was undersold by English competition. The developments in the low-wage countries are the opposite ones, the gaining of industries and jobs, and a surplus in international payments.

The situation just described will be recognized as one that has plagued the United States and other Western nations in the past decade. Industries have shrunken or gone. The people who lost their jobs in these industries have not found comparable jobs elsewhere—there being no large rising industries to take the place of the disappearing ones. Balance-of-payments deficits have been intractable.

These events show why it might be reasonable for China and India to try to bring about such a pattern of developments, and why it would be reasonable for the United States and other high-wage nations to prevent this. The governments of India and China are well aware that their nations suffer from overpopulation. They have tried to limit their overpopulation, which is a difficult matter. But they can escape from the effects of being more overpopulated than other nations—can raise themselves up and pull other nations down so that they are both at the same level—by integrating their economies with those of high-wage nations through international trade.

As the trade equalizes wage rates among the nations involved, lowering those in the West and raising those in China and India, the effects of the overpopulation of those nations will, as it were, be spread equally over all of the nations, and will no longer be a special burden to China and India. With modern transportation and communications, thus, any nation can escape from the effects of its overpopulation, if it can produce effectively for foreign markets. It then ceases to be a separate economic entity, suffering from its own overpopulation, and becomes an element in an integrated world economy, suffering only from world overpopulation to the same degree as other nations. The burden of overpopulation is equalized over the world.

declines in wage rates and living standards

In the next stage in the process, the high-wage nation begins to give in to the pressure of large unemployment, lost jobs, and visibly disappearing jobs by accepting reductions in its wage rates and other incomes. The pressure of lasting unemployment and the seeming absence of prospects for the development of new high-wage jobs causes workers to accept jobs at lower wage rates. Firms that are being undercut by imported goods present their workers with the choice: "Pay cuts or lost jobs." New ways are found, such as bankruptcy proceedings, to get around labor-union contracts that earlier would have been regarded as inviolable. The new need to try to meet the foreign competition brings kinds of actions that would not have been taken in the past.

In the United States and other Western nations in 1983 and 1984, such events gave economic life a quite new flavor. People who a decade earlier thought only of how large a wage increase to demand now found themselves acquiescing in cuts in their wages. Others gave up on getting jobs at their accustomed levels of income and accepted a lower standard of living by taking a lower paid job. On the other end of the process of international economic integration, the low-wage nations enjoyed the process of adjusting to higher wage rates and rapidly expanding new job opportunities.

Similary, governments in high-wage countries found their tax receipts to run ever further below the costs of government programs they had come to take for granted. Local governmental units were thrown into anything-goes competition to attract firms that could bring them jobs and potential future tax revenues. Like people, governments seemed to confront an unwelcome necessity to give up things they had come to think of as permanent dividends of economic growth and progress. Their inability to adjust promptly to the new situation caused large government deficits. These fed back as a factor contributing to the decline of these nations, by squandering on the financing of government deficits the savings that otherwise could have financed productive investment. Here are more conspicuous features of economic life in the West in the 1980s.

trade deficits and exchange rates

The excess of imports over the exports of the high-wage nations has several kinds of effects. The nation that is importing more goods than it exports is, in rather a direct sense, "exporting jobs."[2] As compared with the situation in which the nation's foreign trade is in balance, the nation is producing less and providing fewer jobs for its own people because of the net inflow of goods from abroad—which is providing jobs for people in other countries.

Another effect of the imbalance in international trade, unless it is offset by other factors, is to cause a shift in exchange rates. The excess of imports into the United States over exports tends to cause a decline in the value of the dollar in relation to other currencies.

Such a decline in the international value of the dollar is a means by which the United States cuts the prices of its goods to foreigners, and undertakes to pay higher prices for their goods. What is in question is a change in the "terms of trade." The United States now gives up more goods in relation to what it gets. This worsening of its terms of trade is one channel through which the United States is forced to accept a reduced standard of living. Similarly, the increase in the exchange rate and the improvement in the terms of trade of the nations that are taking over new industries is one of the avenues by which their standards of living are increased.

The decline in the international value of Western currencies and shift of the terms of trade against them has the some of the same effects as a reduction in Western wage rates. Even though money wage rates do not decline, *real wage rates*, or the purchasing power of wage rates can decline through such a shift in exchange rates. The decline in the international value of the dollar means that it costs more dollars to buy imported goods.

The prices of imported goods, measured in dollars, increase. This causes increases in the United States price level, and reductions in the purchasing power of a given level of money wages.

Economics textbooks commonly depict changes in exchange rates as an "adjustment mechanism," in a way that implies a painless adjustment, through which international trade brings benefits to each nation. A nation with a trade deficit, for example, accepts an adjustment in its exchange rate, and all is well. But the reduction in the international value of the dollar, for example, is not a means by which the United States "adjusts" to a deficit in its foreign trade *without pain or cost*. Quite the contrary. It is a means by which the painful and costly "adjustment" of a reduction in its wage rates and standard of living—to bring them into line with the nations with which it is being economically integrated by international trade—are brought about! There is a world of difference between those two interpretations.

The extent of the consequences of a shift in exchange rates, of course, depends on how much of a shift occurs. This is not governed by any general principle, but depends on the specific circumstances of each case. If foreign demand for the nation's exports is elastic—if a small reduction in the foreign price of the goods causes a large increase in the quantity of them bought by foreigners—this will limit the extent of the required shift in the exchange rate and the terms of trade. But in the opposite circumstances, the change in the exchange rate can go very far. If the quantity of goods foreigners buy increases by a smaller percent than the prices decline, the cut in its prices through the decline in its exchange rate makes matters worse, and is self-aggravating. Thus the decline in the exchange rate of the high-wage nation can go very far. Such swings in exchange rates also can be pushed further than they otherwise would go by destabilizing speculation.

The decline in the exchange rate can be limited by an influx of foreign capital, as occurred in the case of the United States in 1983 and 1984. But over a period of time there will be little incentive to move capital into a nation that is losing its industries and slipping downward into second-class economic status. Of course, if the change in the exchange rate goes far enough so that things in the high-wage nation can be bought up at "bargain-basement" prices, this will tend to bring in some funds. But it is not a great boon to the nation to have its firms, its resources, its land bought up by foreigners who are paying only a fraction of what their worth had been, and what their worth could be if the nation adopted policies that protected its interests. With much of its assets in foreign hands, the nation is in a weak position to face the future.

Despite these adverse implications, the deficit in the balance of trade that is paid for, in one way or another, by selling the nation's assets to foreigners is only a way of *postponing* a full reckoning with the changed circumstances of the nation. The nation is thereby able to delay—by using up its capital—making the changes that are required for it to balance its trade with the low-wage nation. Just what this will finally require, again, depends on the circumstances of each case. But in the basic case in which the high-wage nation has no intrinsic or durable production advantages that continue to exist in its new circumstances, what is required is that it make its wage rate and standard of living competitive with that of the low-wage nation with which it has economically integrated itself. The wage rate and standard of living in the low-wage nation will have risen as that in the high-wage nation declined. The decline required of the high-wage nation depends on the sizes of the two nations and the initial discrepancy between their levels of wage rates and living standards.

effects of the decline in the standard of living and the market of the high-wage nation

The process of change under consideration depended on the high standard of living of the high-wage nation. This created the technology and the organizations to produce advanced goods, which then were transferred to or copied by the low-wage nation. It also provided the market for the advanced goods. Shifting the technology and organization to the low-wage nation and shipping the output back to sell in the market of the high-wage nation was a natural result of the economic integration through trade of the two nations.

But this pattern of developments evidently works to destroy the conditions on which it is based. By reducing the standard of living in the high-wage nation, it removes the market for the kinds of goods whose production shifted between nations. It also removes the system within which advanced technology is created. Thus, in taking over the market for advanced products in the high-wage nation, the low-wage nation causes the market to disappear, at least in part. What seems at first, from the viewpoint of the low-wage nation, to be the key to an almost magical spurt of progress proves to be a journey to nowhere, and the economy of the high-wage nation is destroyed along the way.

This pattern of changes involves a great deal of waste. The shift of production from the high-wage to the low-wage nation necessarily wastes capital, skills, and established organizations in the high-wage nation, and causes them to be redeveloped in the low-wage nation. But then these industries prove to be oriented toward a market that will be changing, or disappearing, an additional source of waste. This waste of capital, of organizational capabilities, of established and working economic arrangements destroys powers that under a more constructive structuring of events could have contributed to lasting economic betterment.

This kind of case illustrates how misleading is the emphasis of the orthodox economics on "efficient production" as the criterion for judging economic events. This economics would interpret the shift in production from the high-wage to the low-wage nation as an increase in "efficiency," as decreed by "the price system." But to be realistic, "production" must be considered in its context. Production can continue only if there is a market for the goods produced, which requires a society that can create and sustain such a market. Shifting production away from a society in order to increase economic "efficiency"—at the expense of undercutting the society and the market on which the production depends—is a destructive pattern of events.

Production of a good occurs only where there is a market for it. The existence of the market depends on the standard of living. The standard of living depends on many factors, including the existence of overpopulation, and the character of the nations with which the nation is integrated by international trade. Production depends also on the technology that is relevant and can be used—which depends on the standard of living, which depends on . . . The "production" of which a nation is practicably capable thus depends on a whole set of factors. All of these factors can be radically changed by international trade and international economic integration.

processes caused by the changes in wage rates and living standards

One phase of the process of economic integration through international trade of the high-wage and the low-wage nations could be thought of as complete when the wage rates, standards of living, and other kinds of production standards in the two nations had been about equalized—if some important indirect effects and interaction-processes were ignored. In this incomplete version of the process, the standard of living in the high-wage nation would have fallen and that in the low-wage nation would have risen. The new levels, and the extent of the changes in the two nations, would depend on their relative sizes. If the low-wage nation were much the larger, the new wage level would be near the initial wage level of this country. The low-wage nation would enjoy a modest rise, the high-wage nation a large decline.

But such an interpretation rests on an unjustified assumption of "other things equal," or *ceteris paribus*—which is an essential vice of orthodox economics. This interpretation implicitly assumes that the processes by which the two nations move toward their new situation are "neutral," that the changing conditions do not feed back as causal influences, affecting the process of change, and the direction and scope of the change. Such neutrality cannot be assumed. It is tempting to do so, and the orthodox economics is largely based on this kind of assumption.³ But there is no real basis for assuming that real-world processes somehow operate to generate only the effects we have in mind, or choose to recognize. Realistic analysis must give the uninvited guests, the "side effects," their true place in the drama.

In actuality, the way nations will respond to large changes in their circumstances cannot be predicted. The high-wage nation might fall into political disorder under the necessity of so drastically cutting its expectations and scaling down its commitments. The cumulative processes of deterioration thus generated could cause it to fall even further than was required by its economic integration with the low-wage nation.

The low-wage nation might from its temporary upward movement develop new institutions and attitudes that would then carry it onward to achievements otherwise outside its reach. Or the new wealth might lead to an upsurge in graft, or a break-down of the society's social framework, and throw the nation onto an evolutionary path dominated by problems and destructive causal forces that it did not confront in its earlier state. The processes of change to which nations are subjected by the economic integration will have effects, and these in turn will have their effects. Any realistic analysis must even-handedly take them all into account, as best this can be done. Simply to choose the effects that seem to support a preferred story, and to ignore the effects that do not, is to create a myth.

Also to be taken into account are the implications of the changing situation for the set of goods demanded, the relevant technology, and the ability of the societies to support advanced technology and to generate improved technology and organization. The set of circumstances to which the high-wage nation earlier was adapted, and from which its success derived, is removed by the decline in its standard of living. Earlier achievements in producing advanced goods and developing the knowledge and technology on which this production rested—all of this may now be irrelevant, unusable, to be forgotten in the new situation that has been created.

How the nations will perform in the new situation that is created by the basic economic restructuring cannot be predicted in detail. But it is clear that some of the essential foundations of the success of the high-wage nation have been destroyed by the process of economic integration, and the new economic structure includes formidable impediments to economic advancement, and even to the sustaining of a high standard of living.

effects of national differences in birth rates and rates of population-growth

Finally, there is the potentially all-dominating factor of growth of population. This factor, while present from the first, works on a slower timetable than the other causal elements. If it does become the overpowering factor in determining the outcome of the economic integration, this may be only after some decades have passed.

No simple principles define the role the population factor will play in a particular case. It depends on the circumstances of each case. Population growth unquestionably has the potential power to overbalance all other causal factors and dominate the outcome, bringing about overpopulation-caused poverty throughout the integrated areas. But whether or not this actually happens, and if so how long is required for it to happen, may depend on many circumstances of the case.

A common situation is that a society with a very low standard of living has a high death rate because of malnutrition, poor health care, and other factors. In this kind of case, an increase in the wage rate and standard of living will improve nutrition and health care, reduce the death rate, and cause accelerated growth of population.

What happens when such a nation is economically integrated by international trade with a high-wage, low-birth-rate nation then depends on many causal factors. A large increase in living standards in some cases is accompanied by changes in a nation's attitudes, patterns of life, and social norms that cause a decline in the birth rate and the slowing or halting of population growth. But in other cases, this does not happen, or happens only to a small degree. Differences in cultural and religious factors cause different societies to behave differently in this regard. National differences in laws and institutions also affect the rewards and the costs to parents of having large families. Where governments have explicitly adopted laws and policies aimed at reducing family size and the birth rate, the responses of people and the effectiveness of the programs have varied widely. In general, such programs have not been nearly so effective and politically viable as it was customary to assume a decade or two ago.

The experience of human societies suffering oppressive overpopulation throughout recorded history shows decisively that there is no automatic tendency for human populations to adjust themselves so as to maintain favorable living standards and avoid destruction of the environment. The recent doctrines in which population would be automatically self-regulating if only . . . are only another illustration of false natural-harmony beliefs. Indeed, it would be a great boon to the human species if population were automatically self-regulating, just as it would be a great boon if economies were automatically self-regulating, or if international trade were automatically self-regulating. But the evidence does not support such views, and scientific knowledge of how the world works discloses no way in which such things could happen. If Nature has not preprogrammed a happy outcome, it is reasonable for humans to ask what they must do to avoid an unhappy one.

The durability of high-birth-rate behavior in societies long set in that pattern has been evidenced in many societies. The conflict betweeen low-birth-rate and high-birth-rate ethnic groups has for decades been a major point of conflict in many nations. Nations that desperately need a drastic reduction in their birth rates, and that have undertaken ambitious programs to reduce birth rates, generally have failed to bring about the required large and rapid decline in family size. To achieve some token decline in the birth rate, or some reduction in *the rate of increase in population* may be a considerable accomplishment, but it is not by any means the same thing as halting population growth. The case that merits attention as the most likely one, thus, is that in which a nation with a history of a high birth rate and rapid potential population growth continues for at least some decades to exhibit this behavior when it is economically integrated by international trade with a high-income nation with a low birth rate and substantially stable population—the condition of a number of Western nations. Indeed, the increased wage rates of the low-wage nation may for a time increase its rate of population-growth by reducing its infant mortality and otherwise increasing longevity.

In this case, the levels of wage rates and the standard of living in the economically integrated nations will continue to be pushed downward by the rising population of the high-birth-rate nation. The quantitative force of this depends on the relative sizes of the two populations and the length of time over which the high birth rate persists. Potentially, the high-birth-rate behavior over a period of time comes to dominate the outcome, forcing the standard of living of the integrated nations to a low level.

The decline in the standard of living in the high-wage nation then plays an increasingly important role in the interaction-process. It affects the kinds of goods for which there is a demand, reducing and potentially eliminating the market for advanced goods, the kind of goods that can be afforded only in a society with a high standard of living. The kind of technology and the kind of firms that are tied to the production of such goods thus become increasingly obsolete, irrelevant, as the markets on which they depend disappear. The force that fueled the shifts of industries and jobs to the low-wage nation, to produce for the markets of the high-wage nation, thus weakens and disappears as the high-wage nation becomes a low-wage nation.

Also involved in this process will be the loss by the high-wage nation of other features that depended on its high standard of living: expensive and extended education, elaborate government, high-class utilities, advanced medical treatment, and the availability of trained specialists in science and technology. Moreover, there is the hazard that the downward adjustment in living standards forced on the high-wage nation will throw it into disorder or irrational political actions, which can speed the degenerative processes at work and push them even further than they otherwise would have gone.

In this kind of case, how far does the process of economic deterioration in the high-wage nation go? If the economic integration is retained, and if population-growth in the low-wage nation (or of some substantial group within either nation) continues, in time this process can carry both societies to the kind of backward and impoverished life that is associated with severe overpopulation. For the high-income society, this would be a complete fall, the loss of everything it earlier had gained in economic success, and all of the features of life that depended on it.

As was shown in earlier chapters, what is in question in such a case is an evolutionary process, a complex interaction-process, in which virtually all features of economic life may be changed: the kinds of goods for which there is a market and thus the kinds of goods that are produced, the kind of technology that is relevant and can be used, the level of education and health care, the character of government, the devoting of resources to protection of the environment and to protecting the future of the society—almost everything about life. The process that is potentially in question is the transition from a high-income, technically advanced, knowledge-using society to one that is made backward or "primitive" because of poverty imposed by overpopulation.

It is a distinctive feature of this process that the overpopulation problem can be imposed on a large nation by its economic integration with a small nation. The problem could be imposed on the whole world, in time, even by the integration of relatively small high-birth-rate nations with large stable populations. In the kind of process involved, this is like the spread of an infectious disease. It would require only one person infected with, say, smallpox to cause all of mankind to be subjected to it. The reason for this is the capability of the smallpox virus to multiply at a geometric rate, and thus in time to be able to infect any imaginable number of humans.

Human beings also have the capability of multiplying at a geometric rate, and—though not so quickly as viruses—increasing their numbers beyond any defined limit. Thus a persistent high-birth-rate behavior of a group of people quite dominates the outcome of any group of humans with which this one is economically integrated, even though the high-birth-rate group is initially small. This kind of case thus provides an example of the power of degenerative evolutionary processes to pull advanced societies down to primitivism, and even to inflict this fate upon much of the world.

The disappointing course of events might well cause the high-income nation to question the economic theories that underlay its policies and its acceptance of economnic integration with the low-wage nation. The game would not likely be played out straightforwardly to its bitter end. But neither can it be expected with any confidence that its economic deterioration would bring to the high-wage nation an accurate understanding of what was happening, or a new capability for realistic and rational action. On the contrary, a deteriorating situation is more likely to bring irrationality and group-conflict than illumination and the rule of reason. And it would not be a new experience for a society to go down to oblivion while stubbornly clinging to the delusions that are its undoing.

The lack of understanding in the West of the implications of economic integration between high-wage and low-wage nations has caused it to acquiesce in patterns of trade and losses of its industries that it would not have accepted had a realistic understanding of the matter prevailed. This already has happened to a significant degree. So the West, already overcommitted from its own indiscretions and excessive expectations, wrestles unsuccessfully with the resulting unemployment, deficits in international trade, and seeming inability to support the standard of living and the policies and institutions that have been customary.

The lack of success in coping with this situation, and the seeming worsening of the problems of Western nations, creates a situation whose outcome is very uncertain. Increases in restrictions on imports—even if based on misunderstanding and low motives—may reduce limit economic integration enough to take pressure off Western nations. But political pressures, animosities, and group conflicts arising from the economic pressures can greatly damage the performance of these societies, and accelerate the process of economic decline. There seems to be no basis for a favorable outcome except an increase in understanding of the matter and the general adoption of policies that reasonably protect the interests of each nation and that prevent the further development of the cumulative degenerative processes described.

International Trade in Constructive Evolutionary Processes

Looking now at a brighter evolutionary path into the future, how might international trade contribute to processes of change that promote continued increases in living standards and provide the potential for a higher quality of human life?

A basic requirement is that the course of events generate some cases of success, cases of problem-solving, workable, patterns of successful national economic change, which can inspire and motivate other nations and be copied by them. And these must be successes of *national economies*—and groups of interacting national economies.

World-wide economic success, or the economic success of mankind in general, is not a possibility. All of mankind is not an organization, an operating entity that can succeed or fail. It is the performance of its working organizations, its national economies, that determines which course is taken by that abstraction, "mankind." So long as nations exist in different circumstances, with different cultures and behaviors, moved by different ideologies, and with governments of widely different capabilities following radically different kinds of policies—so long as these conditions exist, nations will generate different kinds of economic performances.

The usual, and only possible, pattern of human economic improvement is one of achievement of successes by some societies, followed by the spread of the improved ways to others. In this, a great many may be in the debt of a few. The subsequent rise of the West, for instance, can hardly be imagined without the basis provided by the achievements of a small group of people in ancient Athens.

In economic achievements, the Hanseatic League played a crucial role as an instigator of and model for the early English steps upward, as well as to other groups. In their period of brilliance in the seventeenth century, the Dutch of Amsterdam were the teachers, exemplars, and goads to the world. The English then continually compared themselves to the Dutch, to their own disadvantage, and resolved to find ways to raise themselves to equal Dutch standards of performance. Peter the Great travelled to Amsterdam, hired many Dutch people to teach his backward Russians—and showed that even copying another nation's economic success may be very difficult.

Similarly, the France of Colbert and Louis XIV was a pattern-setter of its time. And England in the nineteenth century provided the model for other nations in economic development, politics, and other aspects of life. The abrupt rise of Germany made that nation where one went in the late nineteenth century to "learn how" in advanced education, government and administration, science, and technology. For a time after the Second World War—in retrospect, a much shorter time than anyone anticipated—the United States was the leader in management and production. After that, Japan, transforming itself economically with extraordinary rapidity, became the nation to which others looked to learn the new lessons that the times seemed to require. Arrangements for international trade that would prevent or stifle such economic achievements by nations would remove what has been the basis of past economic advance.

But when low-wage nations have the organizational capabilities to use low wages and low standards to win away the attractive industries of the high-wage countries, free trade results in the success of leading nations being undercut, nibbled away, destroyed by this downward-pulling competition. In different circumstances, an opposite kind of difficulty occurs. Where low-wage nations lack the organizational capabilities thus to capitalize on their cheap labor, they are helpless before the organization and technology of the advanced nations, unable to achieve a process of gradual progress because their production is undercut by the experienced and technically advanced nations. This was a problem of other European nations in relation to Britain in its time of dominance, and of many societies in relation to the West in the past two centuries, and in recent decades.

What is wanted is an arrangement for international trade in which both of these difficulties are avoided. The national economic successes are not undermined by low-wage and low-standards competition from other nations, preventing continuing processes of success that can provide a model for mankind. But neither are the successes of nations in advanced positions furthered at the expense of nations that for one reason or another are in less favored positions, which are thereby precluded from developing a cumulative process of economic betterment.

Unregulated private trade across national boundaries, it seems, is an unsuitably unstable arrangement that tends to cause cumulative degenerative processes. In what direction, then, are more constructive arrangements for international trade to be sought?

The obvious starting point, again, is to apply to trade across national boundaries the basic logic of mutualistic economic relations in a world in which the top-level organization is the nation. The nation is the essential and decisive organizing unit of the present economic world. The successes and failures of peoples as nations, in their organizations as nations, provide our terms of reference. The obvious direction in which to look in creating a framework for constructive economic evolution is giving to the nation the responsibilities and powers it requires to protect and develop the interests of its organizational unit, its society, its people.

As the starting point of reasonable consideration of trade across nations' boundaries it must be recognized that nations through their governments have a responsibility for preventing patterns of trade that are detrimental to their interests. The nation should not stand by and let trade across national boundaries that is responsive only to private interests undermine its position and prospects. It should act to assure that its international trade is beneficial to the nation—desirably it should arrange for the most beneficial pattern of international trade its circumstances permit, within suitable rules of fairness to other nations.

It may be objected that under this arrangement nations with advantages of resources, of moderate population density, of traditions of past accomplishments will do better than those that lack them. And nations that have effective, reasonable, intelligent, honest, capable government will do better than nations that do not. But to take these objections seriously is to imply that there is available an arrangement in which this is not true, in which each nation is successful regardless of its policies and its circumstances. That is asking for a miracle, for a situation in which effects do not reflect causes. That is a problem with the orthodox economics, and some other versions of economics. They offer certain rituals—such as leaving things to "the free market"—that assertedly will bring a happy outcome, as it were miraculously, in a way that cannot be given a cause-and-effect explanation.

The first step toward reasonable arrangements for international trade is to recognize that in our world such miracles do not occur. There is no *abracadabra* that permits nations to take whatever kind of actions they wish, lets individuals and firms take whatever actions they wish, and still brings success. The most that can be hoped for in a cause-and-effect world is an arrangement within which those nations that can define and take the required actions can achieve success, and their successes can point the way to further successes for themselves or other nations. The achievements of organized, purposeful, knowledge-using, intelligent human beings are the basis of the past advances of mankind, and the only possible basis of future advances.

6

Truths and Fictions on International Trade

In a cause-and-effect world there are *truths*—statements that accurately describe the effects of causal actions. Reality is what it is. Humans can interpret it honestly and, to a degree, accurately.

But humans have a capability not only for defining truths, but also for creating fictions, myths, appealing stories, optimistic and flattering assertions. These relate not to reality but to wishes, not to the world but to human psychology. The fictions that achieve the greatest and most lasting influence are those stories that serve the purposes of some sponsoring group, tie into a wish or need of people, promise something that people badly want, or justify what a group greatly wishes to justify.

People who base their lives on the belief that the racetrack or the casino will make them rich usually come to a dismal end, their lives ruined by their delusion. Wishes, "dreams," and fictions do not solve problems or achieve goals. In forming their policies, nations similarly confront tempting delusions—

which seem to offer *so much more* than true statements about the world of reality. The consequences of basing actions on flattering delusions are no more favorable for nations than for individuals.

On the subject of international trade, one finds popular and influential doctrines that flatly contradict one another: "Free trade is the best arrangement—the only suitable arrangement." "Unregulated trade may be ruinous to one or both of the nations involved." Which is the truth, and which is fiction? And if a particular fictitious doctrine has been widely believed for decades or centuries, what is it about this fiction, or about the way it is presented, that causes people to find it persuasive? Where is the sleight of hand, the captivating rhetoric, that lends plausibility to doctrines that are inconsistent with experience and with common sense? In getting to the root of matters and laying a solid foundation for a new era of realistic thought about international trade, it is necessary to confront these puzzles.

The Doctrines of Natural Harmony and *Laissez Faire*

The fictions of the *laissez-faire* approach to international trade, or the free-trade doctrine, gain plausibility from the larger fiction of *natural harmony under natural liberty*. This is the idea that things automatically work out for the best when people and firms are "free" to do as they wish.

Usually this approach is presented without explicit justification or rationale. The persuasion comes from the emotional connotations that have been given to the words in which the doctrine is conveyed. To people conditioned to regard "freedom" as the ultimate good, it seems obvious that "free trade" must be desirable. No argument or evidence is needed. When the carrying out of trade across national boundaries is presented as a question of whether people and firms are to have "freedom," it seems obvious where the right lies. Nowadays, many people react with similarly strong positive emotions to "the free market," "competition," and "deregulation," further sealing the case. One finds that in much current discussion of international trade, the use of this emotionally loaded vocabulary is the only persuasion offered, and all that is required. It does the job.

One is reluctant to believe that so large a part in determining the beliefs of the public, and of economists, is played by what is essentially a misuse of language. But there is a decisive test to apply. Reword the familiar—and persuasive—statements in language that is as neutral and as precise as possible. See whether or not the persuasive power remains. If the doctrine no longer seems persuasive, if it now makes no sense, or seems to have no definite meaning, or seems absurd—this tells one something important.

Surely most people would react differently to "free trade" than to "unregulated trade across national boundaries carried out by firms and people pursuing their private interests." When the activity is called "free trade," it seems superfluous, if not inappropriate, to ask: "How does it actually work? What causal processes are operating? What does experience show about the results of this arrangement?"

When the arrangement is described as "unregulated trade ...," it seems that one should inquire how the arrangement actually works, and what experience tells us about its effects. And once these questions are raised, thinking begins to run in a new direction. For there simply is no persuasive explanation of how unregulated trade across national boundaries can be assuredly beneficial to the nations involved. And an objective look at the historical evidence on the matter throws into the face of the observer cases in which such unregulated trade across national boundaries has greatly damaged nations.

Moreover, the concept of "freedom" brings to the minds of most people an image in which people and firms can do as they like—but without giving up any of the taken-for-granted benefits of effective national government, and of firms that produce efficiently, and of a many-sided social framework within which people live. But, again, once one looks behind the verbal images and asks how it is that people can do just as they wish without undermining the effectiveness of government and of firms, without destroying the required social framework of life, there is no persuasive explanation of how such a thing can be. A mere insistence on looking behind the verbal veil brings down the doctrine. Its persuasive power derives from emotionally charged words like "freedom," not from a reasoned interpretation of reality.

The present-day world is of two minds on the question of natural harmony. In fields where people are guided by knowledge and experience, notions of natural harmony are rejected as absurd. The space scientist, the business executive, the engineer, the computer technician, the scientific physician, the football coach would look with incredulity at anyone who told him or her: "Just do X and everything will work out for the best, because Nature planned it all that way." But in popular discussion of economic and political issues, in the orthodox economic theory, in the newly fashionable "natural" formulas for health, the idea that Nature designed the world for human benefit is very influential.

Thus some doctrines on international trade appear to many to be plausible, even seem to be self-evident truths, simply because they are presented within the framework of the natural-harmony view of the world, and in an emotionally loaded vocabulary that people are keyed to accept without question. To distinguish truth from fiction requires removing doctrines from this verbal Neverland, stating them in clear and objective English, considering them in relation to a cause-and-effect world, and inquiring what evidence and experience have to tell us on the point. To do this so alters the appearance of things as to seem almost magical. It removes the word-magic of the natural-harmony myth and lets the victim of that magic see for the first time the world of reality.

Which Freedom? The Anarchistic Bias in the Free-Trade Doctrine

The concept of "freedom," it often has been pointed out, lends itself to misleading and biased interpretations of situations. The various "freedoms" that people define are in many cases inconsistent with one another. Thus the way a situation is interpreted will depend on which "freedom" is recognized and which "freedoms" are ignored.

There is a general conflict between the freedom of each person to do as he or she wishes at the moment, without any constraints or rules, and the freedom of people to form associations and organizations, to run farms and factories, to live in civilized societies. The successful working of, say, an aircraft factory, requires each person engaged in the operation to play out a precisely defined role, do exactly what needs to be done to create an airplane that works—which is quite the opposite of doing just what one wishes at the moment. Straightforwardly applied, the doctrine of individual freedom implies a condition of anarchy.

Though economists may often be a bit loose on this matter, when the issue is raised explicitly they do not favor "freedom" in the sense of anarchy. On the contrary, from Adam Smith on they have emphasized the need for a framework of laws, which are effectively enforced, of property rights that are defended by the government against would-be violators. If the question is raised, they see that an effective economy depends on the ability of the society to establish and rigorously to enforce an elaborate set of rules for economic activities. The imposing of such rules, of course, limits "freedom." Thus economists and economic theory do not really hold for general freedom, or anarchy.

The level of thought and realism in this area has been raised by the new body of economic thought emphasizing the significance of the form of property rights, the role of voluntary contracts and associations among people, and the effect on the performance of an economy of details of the rules and procedures within which economic and political activities are carried out. In bringing out the role of mutualistic contracts and of activities by organized groups, this literature emphasizes the importance of a "freedom" or a "right" that is in a sense the opposite of freedom in the anarchistic sense. This is the right, or the freedom, of people to take coordinated or organized actions on their behalf. In a world of anarchistic individual freedom, this would not be possible. There is a conflict between different kinds of "rights" or "freedoms."

"free trade" as implying the anarchistic kind of "freedom"

It is ordinarily conceded that nations, as organizations or associations of people, need substantial powers if they are to act effectively on behalf of their people. The nation must prevent individuals and firms from doing things that would be in their interest, but would damage the interests of the nation and of other people. Most laws perhaps are designed to prevent people and organizations from taking actions that they wish to take but that will be contrary to the interests of the people of the nation.

Trade across national boundaries can be taken as a typical illustration of such a case. The discussion in Chapter 4 of general externalities in international trade brought out the great divergence of interest between the nation and, say, the consumer who wants to buy imports from a low-wage nation rather than home-produced products, the firm that hopes to undersell its rivals by shifting its production abroad to a low-wage nation.

Given such conflicts of interests, which interests are to prevail? Which voices are to be heard, and which ignored? The free-trade doctrine gives a one-sided, *a priori* answer. It says that those who wish to ship goods across a national boundary must be permitted to do so. What of the interests of those who would be directly or indirectly injured by the trade and the international economic integration? What of the effect on the economic fate of the nation? These considerations are not to enter the picture. The interpretation of the situation is biased in reflecting only one kind of interests, and excluding others. In undercutting rules, policies, and group actions, the free-trade doctrine implements the anarchistic conception of "freedom."

the free-trade doctrine's undercutting of high-income nations

The bias in this doctrine particularly damages high-income nations, and can be ruinous to them. Consider an efficient, low-wage nation and a high-income nation that are seeking to formulate a mutually advantageous package of balanced trade between them. The two nations might have a rough balance in their negotiating positions. The low-wage nation has a bargaining counter in its low wages, which potentially permit it to undersell products produced in the high-income nation. But the high-income nation has a bargaining counter in that its high income gives it a market for many more kinds of goods, and for more advanced goods, than the low-income nation. Access to such markets is needed as the basis for production of advanced goods, and the use of advanced technology, which are important to the improvement of a nation's productive powers. The bargaining assets of both nations would affect the character of a mutually advantageous trade package negotiated between them.

But consider how different the situation is when the free-trade doctrine is applied. The bargaining chip of the low-wage nation still counts. Indeed, the free-trade doctrine gives the low-wage nation a license use its low wage rates to undersell the products of the high-wage nation in other markets and in its home market, and thus take away its industries and its jobs. But the bargaining chip of the high-wage nation no longer counts. Its large market for advanced goods—the result of the set of accomplishments (of gifts of fortune) that underlay its high incomes—now counts for nothing. The high-income nation can get no *quid pro quo* from the low-wage nation for admitting it to this market—a kind of market that the low-wage nation does not have—and which may be essential to its advancement.

The doctrine of "free trade" prohibits the high-income nation from reserving its attractive market for its home industry, and prevents it from receiving a *quid pro quo* as the price of admission to the market of other nations. The free-trade doctrine, in effect, requires the high-income nation to sign a blank check that permits low-wage nations to do whatever they can to invade its markets and take over its industries. Thus the doctrine has an important bias against high-income nations. It implicitly violates the system of mutualistic dealings, or *quid-pro-quo* deals, that are the basis of voluntaristic economies, and of open societies. It provides an extraordinarily important example of the hazard of formulating a general verbal "principle" without considering all of its implications, and all of the kinds of cases to which it might be applied.

In formulating his free-trade doctrine, Adam Smith was thinking mainly in terms of certain cases of his time. He was following the Physiocrats in attacking "Colbertism," or the French "mercantilism" of the time of Louis XIV. Many economists today think of "free trade" also within a limited focus, as the alternative to "protectionism." But deriving a supposedly universal "principle" from this kind of narrow, and biased, consideration is hazardous—and is hardly a model of scientific investigation. The free-trade doctrine has implications that have not been widely recognized, that are inconsistent with other ideas of theoretical economics, and that force an unjustifiably anarchisitic "principle" on human life.

The Fiction that Unregulated Trade Across National Boundaries Is Automatically Beneficial to Both Nations

Orthodox economists since Adam Smith have taken it as a "basic principle" that unregulated trade or "free trade" across national boundaries is automatically, or necessarily, beneficial to both the nations involved. Their argument usually is posed as a refutation of the idea that international trade can damage a high-wage nation by undercutting its wage level and its standard of living. The label usually assigned to the conventional argument is "the principle of comparative advantage" or "the theory of comparative advantage." For an illustrative statement of the doctrine from an authoritative source, we turn to Nobel-prize-winner Paul A. Samuelson:

> International trade is mutually profitable even when one of the countries can produce *every commodity* more cheaply (in terms of labor or all resources) than the other country. Can America with $9-an-hour wages benefit from trade with Japan at $6 an hour? Yes, asserts the theory of comparative advantage. . . .

Whether or not one of two regions is absolutely more efficient in the production of every good than the other, if each specializes in the products in which it has a *comparative advantage* (greatest *relative* efficiency), trade will be *mutually profitable* to both regions. Real incomes of productive factors rise in both places.[1]

This doctrine presents a puzzle. Experience shows that when high-wage labor is thrown into competition with low-wage labor, the low-wage workers take the jobs and the high-wage workers become unemployed—or have to learn to accept low wages to be able to compete. But Samuelson says—stating the conventional doctrine of orthodox economics—that such is not the case when the high-wage and low-wage workers reside in different nations. Indeed, he says it is not the case when they reside in different *regions*.

In cause-and-effect terms, how is it that competition works differently for trade that crosses the boundary of a nation, or even of a region, than for trade that does not? One would suppose that the effects would be the same whether the low-wage and high-wage workers were in the same region or in different ones. How is it argued that competition in international trade or interregional trade is thus automatically beneficial all around, when this is not true of local trade—in which it is agreed that low-wage labor will undercut high-wage labor?

Experience shows, of course, that the argument is not valid. Being undercut by foreign competition has disastrously affected the industries and jobs of many countries, and of regions within countries. The task here is to dissect the conventional argument, to see how the orthodox economics has given plausibility to a doctrine that cannot possibly be correct.

"the principle of comparative advantage" *as a basic error*

Present-day economics depends, on this point, on a line of argument offered by Adam Smith and David Ricardo in the late 1700s and early 1800s. These writers recognized that in the ordinary operation of trade, low costs undercut high costs. This implies that low wages will undercut high wages, and thus will tend to pull them down by causing unemployment in the high-wage area. (Samuelson's assertion that this does not happen in the case of *regions*, as against *nations*, goes beyond what they claimed.) But if this is true, the ordinary working of competition implies that a high-wage nation that opens trade with an equally competent low-wage nation will find its sales and its wage rates undercut, and may be in serious trouble.

This interpretation was inconsistent with the conception that events automatically work out for the best under unregulated trade, which formed the foundation of the economics of Smith and Ricardo. To propound their brand of individualistic economics, they thus were forced to come up with a special justification for unregulated international trade. What they did was to argue that trade across national boundaries works differently than trade within a nation. Within a nation, *absolute costs* govern transactions, and low wages undercut high wages.

But for trade that crosses a national boundary, they asserted, a different "principle" applies. *Comparative costs* or *comparative advantage* then governs events. Low-wage competition does not cause unemployment in the high-wage nation. Rather, both nations come out better off. But, then, there is the question of how this happy result can be caused? What causes trade across a national boundary to work differently than trade within a nation?

The answer that Adam Smith offered, and Ricardo repeated, was that trade worked differently in the two cases because capital, or investment funds, would move freely from one region to another within a nation but would not move across a national boundary. Indeed, it was in this connection that Adam Smith coined his wonderfully evocative metaphor of the "invisible hand" of Nature. What, specifically, the invisible hand did was to implant in businessmen an unwillingness to move their capital across the national boundary, to invest in other countries. In Smith's story, it was only because of this providential peculiarity in the behavior of capitalists—which Nature had foresightedly implanted in them—that international trade was automatically beneficial all around, rather than damaging to nations with high wage rates and high production standards.[2]

On consideration, this argument is untenable, for two reasons. First, as a point of fact, it is not true that capital does not move across national boundaries. It was true to some degree in certain past periods, depending on the circumstances of the times, but by the early 1800s a large volume of capital was moving between nations. In recent decades, capital flows across national boundaries have occurred on an enormous scale. On this score, even if Adam Smith's argument were valid, it ceased to be factually applicable more than 150 years ago.

But, second, the argument is not valid. The refusal of capital to cross national borders would not suffice to cause the outcome that Smith, Ricardo, and present-day orthodox economics claim would occur. If English capital will not cross the border and move to Portugal—to use Ricardo's classic example—that does not prevent trade between low-wage Portugal and high-wage England from having disastrous effects on England. Given a substantial wage advantage, the Portuguese can produce for export and undersell English goods in the English market and in international markets without any need of British capital. There is no rule that production that undersells British competition must be financed with British capital. The Portuguese can expand production with their own capital, which will increase rapidly as they undersell the British and enjoy booming sales. On the other end of the deal, English capital will disappear because of the losses of the undersold English firms. To take a modern example, Japan did not need American capital to undersell American production, but did it with its own capital.

Of course, if Portugal were afflicted with severe production inefficiencies—were incapable of saving, or of running efficient firms, or were incapacitated by corruption or violence—then these production incapabilities could offset its wage advantage, so it would be no threat to the English standard of living. But that kind of case does not support "the principle of comparative advantage," or the assertion that international trade works differently than intranational trade. It only supports a "principle" such as: "If a low-wage nation is prevented from producing efficiently by other circumstances, then its low wages will not pose a threat to the standard of living of a high-wage country." But that point is commonplace, and it applies in exactly the same way to trade within a nation as to trade across national boundaries.

where's the error? the unrecognized assumption that international trade is automatically balanced

The argument that has been offered to justify the assertion that international trade works diffrently than trade within a nation is, it seems, not applicable to present-day conditions, and is in any case invalid. But, then, one wonders, just what is going on here? How can this erroneous doctrine have achieved the status of one of the ideas on which economists are most in agreement? What *underlies* this so-often-repeated assertion?

The principle of comparative advantage ordinarily is presented, and is thought about, on the basis of a hypothetical example. What is shown in this imaginary case is that even though Portugal, for example, has low wage rates and England high wage rates there still can be defined packages of trade between the two nations that would benefit both of them. As Samuelson puts it, "If each specializes in the products in which it has a *comparative advantage* . . . trade will be *mutually profitable* to both regions."[3]

The critical point is what is omitted from this statement that is required to make it correct. "Trade will be mutually profitable" *if, and only if, what?* In the posing of these illustrative examples, it is implicitly assumed that the trade between the nations *is in balance and is in balance on terms that are beneficial to both nations.* "You grow bananas and we'll grow oats; we'll arrange a deal between the two nations that will make both nations better off." That is an interesting case—but it is not the case of "free trade." That is a case of prearranged trade between the governments of two nations, which is arranged to be balanced, and balanced on terms that are beneficial to both nations.

Consider the effects of unregulated private trade under circumstances in which Portugal could grow both bananas and oats cheaper than England. Portugal then undersells England in both goods. Portuguese farm workers now have new jobs producing for the English market. English farm workers lose their jobs. England has a deficit in its international payments and Portugal has a surplus. A process then is set in motion that, as has been shown in earlier chapters, can radically alter the positions of both nations, and can be ruinous to England.

Deriving generalizations from hypothetical cases is a touchy business. Unless accurate thought is applied, the conditions under which the generalization is applicable can be misstated. That is what has happened in this case. Two major conditions that must be met if the trade is to be beneficial to both nations are (1) that the trade be in balance—so it does not cause a net shift of industries and jobs between nations and a long chain of consequences of this—and (2) that the trade must be balanced on terms that benefit both nations—so one nation does not gain the rewarding industries and the other one get stuck with the losers.

These two conditions will be assuredly met only when the trade is purposefully arranged by the governments of the two nations. There is no way in which this outcome can result from the myopic and self-serving dealings of private firms and individuals. The expected result of individualistic trade is that it will not be in balance, which will damage one nation, and that the industries in which one nation specializes will be more desirable than those that fall to the other. There also are other potential problems, which were discussed above, standards-lowering competition, instability, national dependency, and so on.

What particular feature is it in the example used by Smith, Ricardo, and present-day orthodox economists that causes them to derive the false "principle" that international trade works basically differently than intranational trade and automatically is beneficial to both nations? It seems that they implicitly consider only hypothetical examples in which trade between the nations is *in balance*, and ignore the point that trade ordinarily would not be in balance. The high-wage nation will find its goods generally undersold, its jobs disappearing, its international payments in deficit, and a seriously threatening chain of events occurring.

The error of failing to see these things is explained in part by the view of the orthodox economists that the way to derive "principles of economics" is to consider an idealized, hypothetical economy that does not use money. They viewed money as a "veil" that obscured the true, universal principles. Following this false guideline, they consider international trade as if it were a nonmonetary, or barter, deal. If it were, of course, the trade between two nations would be in balance. Goods would be exchanged only for other goods. But this is not the situation that exists, or that existed in Adam Smith's time. A false "principle" was created by generalizing from an unrealistic hypothetical case.

Another source of the error is the careless use of language. It is common to refer to trade across national boundaries as trade, say, between "England" and "Portugal." This is misleading, because the trade is not between the two nations, as nations, but between individuals and firms, which need not even belong to the nations involved. Economists seem to have been misled by their metaphor, and to have gone on to reason: "Trade between England and Portugal would not occur unless both England and Portugal agreed to it, and they would not have agreed to it unless they benefitted from it. Thus, it follows that international trade—"free trade"—must in all cases be beneficial to the participating nations."

But as we have seen, "England" and "Portugal" have no role in determining the transactions that cross their borders under unregulated, individualistic trade. The economists who reasoned in this way were too loose in their use of language, and were misled by their own words.

This is a case rather like the Emperor's clothes. For two hundred years, economists have been determinedly seeing something that does not exist. "The principle of comparative advantage" and the assertion that international trade works basically differently than intranational trade are falsehoods.

The Fiction that All International Trade Increases Production Efficiency

The orthodox economics treats international trade as if it necessarily led to increases in production efficiency. All international trade is viewed as like what might be termed the oats-and-oranges case: "Cold Scotland is suited for growing oats. Sunny Spain is good for growing oranges. The production will be more efficient if Scotland grows all the oats and Spain grows all the oranges, and they then exchange. Because of the additional production efficiency, it will be possible to arrange a deal whereby both nations will be made better off by the specialization and exchange."

All of this is unobjectionable. But it then is common to add, which is not correct, "and *any* trade that actually occurs between Scotland and Spain will be based on production efficiency and beneficial to both countries." We recall that ordinary trade is arranged between private parties and is not necessarily beneficial to both nations, or to either nation, once the indirect effects are taken into acount.

But it is important to go further and recognize that international trade may have a basis very different than the oats-and-oranges case. It may have no justification in real economic efficiency. When England and other nations took away the textile industry of the North Italian towns, to their ruination, did this reflect some inherent superiority of England over Italy in the production of textiles? When the electronics and camera industries and much of the automobile industry shifted from the United States to Japan, was that because these industries were inherently more efficient in Japan than in the United States?

No, surely not. The oats-and-oranges case, in which each country produces goods for which its climate or resources give it an advantage, is largely limited to agriculture and mining. Factories for manufactured goods can be built anywhere. One basis of technical efficiency is locating factories where transportation costs are minimized. But on that basis, the automobile factories were more efficient in the United States, near their largest market and needed raw materials, than in Japan. It is technically efficient to grow oranges in Spain rather than in Scotland, but it is not technically efficient to produce goods in Japan for the markets of the United States and Europe.

One often sees it asserted that shifts of industries among nations caused by differences in costs and prices necessarily reflect considerations of "efficiency," implying that these are like the oats-and-oranges case. In truth, many such shifts, if not most, are of a quite different character. Industries can move from one nation to another even when technical efficiency is reduced. What, then, motivates the shift? It is motivated, of course, by profit, by cost-avoidance, but the avoidance of costs does not necessarily imply an increase in efficiency.

It is profitable to shift an industry to Taiwan or South Korea because wage rates are lower there—even though the increased transportation costs imply a reduction in technical efficiency. So international trade is motivated not only by technical efficiency, but also by differences in wage rates, and in production standards and regulations, and in all of the other factors that affect money costs. Production moves from high-cost labor to low-cost labor, and from high production standards to lax, cost-saving production standards.

Our earlier discussion brought out the ambiguity of the concept of "efficiency" as applied to changes in the degree of international economic integration and the pattern of production. From a cost-minimization viewpoint, the most "efficient" arrangement is production using workers who are paid the minimum amount necessary to keep them alive. And in trade and competition based on costs, this is the kind of "efficiency" that counts—low-wage rates *do* undercut high wage rates.

But producing goods with impoverished people in order to produce at low cost is not "efficiency" of the kind that is to be sought through international trade and international economic integration. What is wanted here is "efficiency" in creating and sustaining high standards of living, high production standards, and advanced or civilized human societies. What contributes to this kind of "efficiency" is arrangements that create high wage rates, not low wage rates. On important questions, the two ways of thinking, and the two concepts of "efficiency," are the opposite of one another.

The orthodox economics has not made these distinctions. It has used the conception of "efficiency" too loosely. It has generally *assumed* that the kind of "efficiency" that is promoted by the profit motive, by self-serving individual actions and cost-saving competition, is the *only* kind of efficiency and is necessarily beneficial. On consideration, it is obvious that this is a dangerous error.

In interpreting international trade and the related shifts of industries among nations, it must be kept in mind that there exist fundamentally different kinds of trade packages and situations. The oats-and-oranges case does not represent international trade in general, but only a special situation. International trade can confer private profit even though it is a zero-sum or negative-sum game from the viewpoint of the nations involved, or of mankind in general. Much that is written on international trade assumes it is necessarily a positive-sum activity from the viewpoints of the nations and of people in general. This is another fiction.

The Fiction that Free Trade Provides the Optimal World Allocation of Resources, and Maximizes World Output

Another element in the support of *laissez faire* trade across national boundaries by orthodox economics is its assertion that this arrangement brings the optimal allocation of world resources (makes the best possible use of world resources) and thus makes world output as great as it can be. For a succinct statement of this idea, we turn again to Professor Samuelson:

> Free trade promotes a mutually profitable regional division of labor, greatly enhances the *potential* real national product of all nations, and makes possible higher standards of living all over the globe.[4]

This important proposition—a foundation doctrine of the orthodox, individualistic economics—merits consideration from several perspectives.

the assumption that unregulated trade increases production efficiency

We note that this generalization rests on the assumption, or the assertion, that individualistic trade necessarily increases production efficiency. That is, the doctrine assumes that all trade across national boundaries reflects the oats-and-oranges case, rather than the low-wages-undercut-high-wages case. In other words, this proposition is a manifestation of the the general fiction that individualistic actions governed by prices effectuate a constructive "efficiency," rather than a cost-saving "efficiency" that can lead to human degradation.

the gain in "efficiency" from equalizing world incomes

From a certain viewpoint taken by the orthodox economics, it can be said that equalizing incomes throughout the world would increase "efficiency." Thus, Samuelson asserts that the movement of people from a low-wage country to a high-wage country will tend "to increase *total* world production. Because the transfer of workers from their poor Belgian farms to rich American farms would increase their labor productivity and would increase total world output."[5]

It is understood in this kind of case that the increase in the "labor productivity" of the Belgians will be the counterpart of a decline in the "labor productivity" of the Americans (these are "marginal productivities," the reader familiar with this terminology will note). This kind of change does not make the workers in both nations better off. It makes the workers in one nation better off and those in the other one worse off.

On certain assumptions that are frequently used in the orthodox economics, however, such a development would increase aggregate world income—even though it lowered the incomes of Americans. But it must be kept in mind—economists often forget this—that what is asserted is not that such a development would *really* increase world income, but that it would increase world income *ceteris paribus*. It would increase world income if the shift of people occurs *but other factors do not change*. But here, again, is the joker in this kind of theoretical economics. The other things that the theory conventionally holds unchanged, in fact, *will not be unchanged*. Thus, it is not at all inconsistent to say that such a movement of people "will increase world output, *ceteris paribus*," and to say that it "will lower world living standards and make for world poverty."

How can these seemingly inconsistent statements both be true? There is no inconsistency. For one thing, an increase in world income is not inconsistent with a reduction in world standards of living. An increase in population commonly would cause an increase in aggregate output and income, and a reduction in income per person and in the standard of living. It is important here to distinguish between aggregate income and income per person.

Another reason why there is no inconsistency is because the two statements refer to two quite different cases. The case often referred to by the orthodox economic theory is that in which aggregate world income increases *if world population is unchanged, and the technology in use is unchanged, and production methods are unchanged, and resources per person are unchanged*. But, as we have seen in earlier chapters, the shift of people or of industries among nations does not leave these variables unchanged. The movement of people between countries can increase world population (in this connection, little Belgium is perhaps a misleading case; consider rather India or China). The reduction in the standard of living in high-income countries will reduce or eliminate the market for advanced goods and the use of advanced technology—and so on through the many causal links discussed in earlier chapters.

Within the *ceteris paribus* framework of orthodox economic theory, it generally is true that "efficiency" is increased by eliminating "barriers" of any kind, and by permitting full economic integration of all nations. But this conclusion requires the *ceteris paribus* framework, which cannot be asserted to be realistic, to describe the patterns of events that actually will occur. When the variables that had been artificially held unchanged are permitted to change, and interactive evolutionary processes are recognized to exist, a quite different picture emerges. The static "efficiency" then is seen to be applicable only in very special cases, and otherwise a seriously misleading guide to the way the world works.

the fiction of hypothetical world "equilibrium income"

The crowning achievement of the orthodox, individualistic, economics commonly is viewed by its proponents as being its *general equilibrium theory*. This relates to an imaginary economy that is in a full state of equilibrium and adjustment to its governing conditions. This model, or theoretical fiction, is used by asserting the system's behavior to be governed by certain "functions" of conventional form, and predicting what will happen if one factor changes while others are held unchanged.

Though economists think of this kind of theorizing as revealing "principles" about the real world, it is more realistically viewed as revealing the implications of the model or theory, of the particular imaginary world that is created. This particular imaginary world is one in which there are no highly interactive evolutionary processes. It is a *ceteris paribus* kind of world, in which factors are independently determined, and interaction among factors and chain-reaction evolutionary processes do not occur. In this spirit, its imaginary human beings do not learn from experience, copy one another, exhibit fads and fashions, commit follies, reflect changing culture and institutions. Rather, they independently, rationally, mechanically set about filling a set of in-built "economic wants" that are unaffected by experience. The destiny and mission in life of these hypothetical "humans" is to maximize the filling of fixed and given "economic wants."

In this hypothetical world, how do things work out for the best? Why, when each person is *free* rationally to maximize the filling of his or her in-built economic wants. The generalization fits the model. But it is not a statement about the world. It is a statement about the characteristics of this kind of hypothetical model.

The important thing to thing to see about the assertion of the individualistic economics that the "optimal equilibrium position" and "maximization of world income" are achieved under "free trade" and "the free market" in a world with minimum activites of government is that this is not an experience-supported statement about the way the world works. It does not relate to the world of reality. It is a statement about a certain model, a set of beliefs, an ideology. To the actual world, and actual economies, these conceptions have no demonstrated applicability.

For the actual world and actual economies are governed by evolutionary processes in which all of the variables interact and change. They are inhabited by creatures that have very little in common with the mechanical, individualistic utility-maximizers of economic theory, creatures that are themselves not fixed and given, but are also a variable in the evolutionary processes in question. How human beings are to live in the decades and centuries ahead—what, in effect, human beings are to *be*—is perhaps the most basic point at issue.

The Fiction of "the Productivity of the American Worker"

Another popular argument for "free trade" has been that the high wages, for example, of the American worker are not threatened by imports from low-wage nations because they reflect the superior "productivity" or "efficiency" of the American worker. As the point is made by Samuelson:

> High American real wages come from high *efficiency*, not from tariff protection. Such high wages, the *result* of productivity, do not handicap us in competing with foreign workers.[6]

Such statements imply that American workers somehow have built into them a superior "productivity" or "efficiency." This in-built superiority, it is implied, is what causes them to receive higher wage rates than people of other countries. And since this productivity or efficiency is an inherent, unchanging, permanent feature of the American workers, they need not fear competition from low-wage foreign labor.

These statements also imply that low-wage workers in another country receive low wages only because they have built into them a low productivity or efficiency. The low productivity that causes their low wage rates thus prevents them from undercutting high-wage, and high-productivity, American workers. Individualistic trade across national boundaries thus poses no threat to the wage rates and standard of living of high-wage nations.

Until recently, many Americans, including economists, seemed really to believe that Americans had some innate superiority over other peoples. Americans could do things that could not be done by Japanese, Italians, or Chinese. Although the argument lingers on in economics textbooks and policy discussions, surely the belief that underlay it has been refuted by the experience of recent decades. Recent remarks on worker superiority more commonly raise the question whether American workers can match the high standards set by Japanese workers.

Obviously, this doctrine of "the superior productivity of the American worker" has proved to be a misleading guide to events. It presented a false picture of the effects of international trade. In fact, low foreign wage rates did cause, and are causing, the undercutting of American production and American jobs. What has happened is precisely what this doctrine claimed would not happen. Experience has shown it to be a falsehood, a fiction. Just where does its error lie?

The error here is another example of the misinterpretation by the orthodox economics of "efficiency" and "productivity." It was *assumed* that if a group, such as American workers, received an unusually high income, this implied that they were more "efficient" or "productive" in some *fundamental* sense, which *justified* their receiving the high wages. This interpretation fits into the picture of everything automatically working out for the best under "the free market."

In actuality, Americans earned high incomes producing steel, automobiles, machinery and many other kinds of products not because of any in-built characteristics of these industries—and surely not because of any in-built and unique characteristics of American workers. They earned high incomes because these products were in strong demand, in short supply, and there then existed very little competitive productive capacity in other areas of the world. In other words, Americans earned high incomes because the rewarding industries of the times were located in the United States. And these were rewarding industries because they were subject to little foreign competition, and to no efficient, low-wage competition.

As the building of steel mills became fashionable—perhaps from the misapprehension that making steel was a uniquely "productive" activity—steel came to be in excess supply, overcapacity prevailed in the industry, plants stood idle, firms failed, and workers were unemployed. The industry was no longer rewarding. The high "productivity of American steel workers" disappeared.

As the peculiar circumstances of the years after the Second World War that virtually exempted United States firms and workers from foreign competition in major industries were replaced by more normal conditions, and as international trade and international economic integration mushroomed, the United States found itself increasingly undercut by foreign industries. These had a decisive cost advantage over American firms. Their workers received lower wage rates, and they were in some cases as "productive" as, or even more "productive" than, the American workers. Undercut by foreign production, the United States lost industries and jobs.

What happened, then, to the "productivity" of the American workers that had been employed in these industries? It vanished. It was not really "the productivity of the American worker" but "the productivity of the X industry under the peculiar conditions of the times." The productivity moved with the industry. It became "the productivity of the Japanese worker, or the Taiwanese worker." Or the "high productivity" vanished as the industry became subject to low-wage competition or to excess capacity.[7]

The United States, secure in the false knowledge that its economic position was protected by "the productivity of the

American worker," played in this game the role of the sitting duck. It sang paeans to "free trade" while its production and jobs were undercut by low-wage production in other nations, while the industries on which its full employment and its standard of living were based moved to other nations.

The doctrine of "the productivity of the American worker" was misleading, an error, a fiction. The error derived from a misinterpretation of "efficiency" and "productivity," a kind of error that is characteristic of natural-harmony economics. Governed by the preconception that incomes reflect "productivity"—in some ill-defined but justificatory sense—economists argue backwards, asserting "productivity" to be whatever it *must* be to "explain" the level of wages that exists. Realism requires an escape from such muddled and biased concepts. We know that realism in such matters is not beyond the capabilities of human beings. Some nations seem to have known exactly what *they* were doing.

The Fiction that Economic Success Depends Only on Production Capabilities

One reason why the orthodox economics has developed so false a picture of the implications of international trade and international economic integration is because it has treated the nation's economic welfare as depending only on its production capabilities—which are assumed to depend on resources and production techniques that are independently given.

Little attention thus is paid to the role of demand as a determinant of production, and of many factors, including the population situation, as determinants of demand. Account is not taken of the consideration that the only goods that can be produced are those for which there is a demand. And the ability of a nation at any time to produce a good depends on its past experience at producing it—which depends on its past demand for it, which depends among other things on the pattern of international trade.

Orienting economics thus one-sidedly to production was one of the innovations of Adam Smith, two centuries ago. The orthodox economics retains this approach virtually unchanged. The die is cast, as it were, in the opening sentence of *The Wealth of Nations*:

> The annual labour of every nation is the fund which originally supplies it with all the necessaries and conveniencies of life which it annually consumes, and which consist always either in the immediate produce of that labour, or in what is purchased with that produce from other nations."[8]

A great deal is said in this sentence. First, a nation's output is determined by its economic inputs. Smith first toys with counting only labor as an input, but then includes land and capital, making the last the major determining factor.

Second, these economic inputs are taken as given, and not as depending significantly on past experience, on demand as the determinant of the nation's past production experience, or the pattern of international trade as a determinant of its demand and its production.

Third, international trade is treated as if it involved a barter exchange of goods between nations, rather than money dealings by self-serving firms and individuals—a fateful error.

The approach to economics that Smith here set into surprisingly long-lived concepts did not take into account that for a good to be produced, or for a production process to be used, there must be a market for the output! This economics takes the availability of markets for granted, treats demand as a passive and unimportant element in the subject. One reflection of this biased view of the economy was the dominance of faith in Say's law, which says that "supply creates its own demand."

The inference from this doctrine that since has received most attention is the view that there can never be a general deficiency of demand for an economy's output, no "general glut," and no depression or economic slack. On this point, the doctrine is no longer accepted, though it could not be said that there has been achieved a nice agreement as to exactly what is wrong with it.

But this approach to economics is subject to a more basic and broader criticism, which is brought out by observing that there is at least as much truth in the opposite statement: "Demand creates its own supply." Where there is an effective demand for a thing, someone will produce it—if necessary, inventing a way to produce it. On the other hand, if there is no demand, the good will not be produced, even if the means of producing it are at hand, and new ways of producing it will not be developed, even if the potential for doing so exists.

To an important extent, then, it is demand that determines what is produced, and what is produced determines what lines of production and what skills and facilities are developed in the nation. It is this past experience that determines what production capabilities a nation actually has at any point in time. In an important sense, demand determines what is produced, and what is produced determines what the nation is capable of producing.

The effective demand for the various kinds of output of a nation depends on the existing pattern of international trade. The critically important competition among nations for the leading or promising industries of the times is essentially a competition for control of world *demand* or *market* for the goods in question. The nation that enjoys the benefits of the industry is the nation that is able to put itself into the position of capturing, or filling, that demand. So the *demand* that plays so important a role in the economic rise and decline of nations is not only the domestic demand—susceptible as this is to the influence of policies and institutions—but also the particular foreign demand that falls to the nation because of the prevailing pattern of international trade. In setting up economics as he did, Adam Smith managed to leave out this side of the picture—which he had to do if international trade was to be depicted as automatically beneficial to all nations.

When a searching look is taken at the differences in production patterns and production capabilities of various countries and different eras, it becomes clear that it is demand that mainly calls the tune. A great many things *could be* produced. The pattern of demand determines which ones *are* produced. Gothic cathedrals could be produced now—if a demand for them existed. Surely there now exist the counterparts of those men and women who created the great literature of Victorian England, but there is little demand now for such things. Paintings like those of Raphael could be created now—and surely paintings like those that comprise "modern art" were not beyond the capabilities of Raphael, Leonardo, or Michaelangelo. It was demand that determined which of the countless things that could have been done actually were done.

An important illustration of the misleading effects of thinking that current production potential is the only limitation on economic advancement is the misinterpretation of the sources and the implications of the economic lead of the United States over the rest of the world, say, from the 1930s to the 1960s. This was attributed to an assumed ability of the United States to produce things that other nations and other peoples were incapable of producing. This assumption lay behind the once-prevalent boasts that the United States had X percent of the world's automobiles, Y percent of its telephones, and Z percent of its refrigerators. It also lay behind the explanations of this situation by economists and others in terms of "the superior productivity of the American worker."

Events have shown that what lay behind this situation was not a unique production capability of American workers or factories, but a set of circumstances that could change quickly, and that did so. The United States had substantially higher wage rates and standard of living than other countries during several decades because of a combination of circumstances—a very favorable land-to-people ratio, extraordinary resources, having economically benefitted from rather than being ruined by the World Wars, the temporary lack of foreign competition in rewarding manufacturing industries, and so on.

During this period, its higher standard of living made the United States *the first nation to have a mass market for a new generation of pattern-setting industrial goods, automobiles, refrigerators, washing machines, and so on.* Being the only nation with a demand for them, and thus the first to produce them on a large scale then made the United States the first seller of these mass-produced goods in the markets of other nations, as these developed with improvements in their standards of living. It was the unique demand situation of the United States that led to the development of its production capabilities, which then had further effects.

But the situation changed quickly after the Second World War. Other nations developed industries to produce for sale in the United States market, and the world market. The ability of other nations to produce these goods as efficiently as the United States—to an embarrassing extent, better than the United States—quickly became apparent, but the implications of this have not been thought through.

Because they interpreted the economic dominance of the United States after the Second World War as reflecting unique production capabilities, economists worried that the United States would forever stand high above other nations, which would suffer a permanent "dollar shortage" because they could never compete with the United States in production. Events, of course, did not follow this pattern.

Other nations rapidly undercut United States production in many lines with their lower wage rates and sometimes superior capabilities. They invaded the United States market and forced United States firms to shift production to other countries to match their prices and avoid failure. The United States acquired the symptoms of an economically declining nation: the loss of industries, of jobs, the deficits in international trade.

The unique economic position of the United States thus is disclosed as having rested on its higher standard of living, with its unique market for advanced goods being tapped almost entirely by its domestic industries—conditions that depended on circumstances and proved temporary. Neglect of the role of demand as a determinant of production, and thus of current production capabilities, underlay the prevalent misinterpretation of these events.

The neglect of demand and its implications that is built into the orthodox economic theory causes a similarly misleading picture of the potential developments of the decades ahead. United States support of unregulated, individualistic international trade still rests on the notion that the high United States standard of living derives from inherent production advantages, which cannot be damaged by international trade. Once it is recognized that the period of economic superiority of the United States did not rest on production advantages that were in-built or unchanging but on a uniquely favorable situation of demand, the potential events of coming decades present a quite new appearance. The demand advantage of the United States does not accrue to the nation's benefit under unregulated international trade. The inherent production advantage never existed. In open international competition, low wage rates undercut high wage rates. Rather than being secure, the economic position of the United States under these rules appears untenable.

More broadly, the neglect of the importance of demand of the orthodox economics leads it to deny the potentially dominant influence of the population factor in the world economic developments of coming decades. The world-wide spread of the effects of overpopulation works in part through altering the level of incomes, the pattern of demands, the kinds of goods that can be produced, and thus the technology that actually can be used—and the "marginal productivities" of all factors of production.

What mankind *could have produced*, the wonderful technology the species *could have created*, count for nothing at all in a world with a universally low standard of living because of overpopulation. The great things that might have happened if . . . will not happen. What might have been accomplished will not be accomplished. All of this will remain unknown, in the realm of "what might have been." These are some of the things the orthodox economics has managed to leave out of its view of the world through its neglect of the role of demand as a determinant of the character of economic life.

Again, the Fiction of "Free Trade" *or* "Protectionism"

In a listing of major fictions about international trade, it is necessary to mention a point discussed earlier, the fiction that the only choice available is between "free trade" and "protectionism." In truth, many different approaches to international trade are possible, and many exist. Indeed, it is reasonable to argue that neither "free trade" nor "protectionism" is worth talking about in a serious discussion of national economic policy.

The dependence of the misleading past discussion of this subject on the simple misuse of language, the simple verbal fiction, of "free trade" or "protectionism" is almost impossible to overstate. If economists were required to strike from their writings and their thinking the propagandistic concept, "protectionism," they would find themselves near to empty handed. Those seeking a realistic interpretation of international trade need to keep in mind this dominance of the discussion by the misuse of language.[9]

Fictitous Explanations for the Plight of the West—With their Remedies

The popular explanations of the economic plight of the United States and the West have been shaped by the orthodox economics. In interpreting the great shifts of industries and of the economic positions of nations of recent decades, most interpreters have taken for granted that free trade is necessarily beneficial to the nations involved, that "adjustment mechanisms" will make everything work out for the best, that a lack of economic success of a nation must reflect deficiencies of its "productivity" or "efficiency." Most of these economists *know* that the plight of the United States and the West cannot reflect their industries being undersold by low-wage foreign competition—because they have been taught "the principle of comparative advantage."

Approaching the recent events within a false theoretical framework leads necessarily to the creation of a set of fictional explanations of events, and of false remedies. The situation can be likened to the explanations of illnesses that were offered before the discovery of bacteria and viruses. Having no knowledge of the true cause of a wave of illness, people had to "explain" it by inventing false causes. In such situations, each faction invents a cause that fits in with its preconceptions. Religionists say the illnesss is punishment for sins. Food faddists say it is from eating too little, or too much, of X, and so on through the inventory of belief-groups.

So with the plight of the West. It is being attributed to excessive government regulation, to be cured by "deregulation;" to insufficient activities by government, to be cured by "industrial policy;" to old-fashionedness and "smokestack industries," to be cured by the shift to a new generation of industries, variously defined; to deficiencies in "productivity," for which each faction has its own explanation and cure. Almost every conceivable cause shows up in the sweepstakes—but rarely the actual cause.

the West's problem is that it did not have an "industrial policy"

One reading of the situation is this: "Japan has been the winner in this game. Japan had an industrial policy to target desired industries. The United States and the West have done badly because they did not have industrial policies. Thus, the remedy is for the West to adopt industrial policies."[10]

A critical factor that is missing in this interpretation is the great cost advantage that Japan and other efficient low-wage nations had over the United States and the West. It was this cost advantage that permitted them to undersell Western products in Western markets and world markets. It was this underselling of Western products that caused the shift of industries and jobs to the East, and caused the plight of the West. This power to undersell Western industries also put Japan and its companion nations in a position to raise to themselves the question: "Since we have the power to undersell Western products and take their industries, what particular industries will it be most rewarding to us to take from them?" The ability to undersell the West created a basis for having an industrial policy.

When the role of cost differences is thus understood, it becomes clear that industrial policy cannot be expected to do for the United States what it did for Japan. The nation that has high costs because of its high wage rates and standard of living (and other factors) and that is being undersold by other nations is not in a position to pick which industries it wishes to take over by underselling foreign competition. It is on the other side of the fence. Its "industrial policy" will work differently, will be a very different kind of thing.

Government actions to try to hang onto desired industries in which the nation is being undersold by foreign production may in some cases be justified. But subsidizing such industries requires raising taxes or government borrowings, which piles additional cost burdens on other industries. An undiscriminating "save-our-industries-through-subsidization" kind of "industrial policy" embarked on by a nation that is being undersold by low-wage foreign competition is not a promising venture. And, again, such a program is surely not what caused the Japanese success.

The effects and the potential of industrial policy thus can only be seen realistically in relation to an accurate understanding of the role of costs, and national wage levels, in determining patterns of international trade. Ascribing the Japanese success to its industrial policy and inferring that industrial policy thus will do the same thing for the United States, or France, or Britain is a basic and important error.

But governments that came to understand the dangers of a trade deficit caused by low-wage foreign competition and to arrange for balance in their international trade would face the question of "industrial policy," in a broad sense, in a quite different setting. In arranging for its international trade to be in balance, such a government would have to approve the kinds of goods the nation would import and export, and thus would confront the issue of the international location of industries.

Once it is accepted that the self-seeking dealings across national boundaries of individuals and firms do not protect the interests of the nation, it becomes clear that in a basic sense the nation must have an industrial policy. But this is not the same "industrial policy" that is the stereotypic cause of the Japanese success—which some are proposing for the United States and the West. A correction of the theoretical framework and reinterpretation of the causes of recent economic events seem to be essential prerequisites for a realistic discussion of various versions of "industrial policy."[11]

getting the with-it industries— beyond "the new frontier"

Another popular approach is to ascribe the failure of the West and the rise of Japan to the particular industries involved. The West is in trouble because it did not go into the right industries. The answer, logically, is for it to go into them now. Then there is the question of what *are* the industries that will be laying those golden eggs in the future.

This view and the preceding one, it must be noted, are not straightforward applications of the orthodox economics, but involve a degree of heresy. For neither proposes to leave the pattern of international trade and the international location of industry to be determined by "the free market." Both propose that government should attempt to influence what industries the nation develops.

But though heretical in this respect, these views are orthodox in assuming that there must be a cure for the plight of the West within the framework of generally individualistic international trade. Some accept the view that low-wage foreign competition poses no threat to a high-wage nation—as "the principle of comparative advantage" says. Others, however, observe that it is its cost advantage that permits foreign production to undercut American production, and that the low wage rates in other nations are the major source of this cost advantage. Implicitly—though they do not draw the needed inferences from the point—they observe from experience that *low-wage foreign industries do undercut high-wage Western industries.*

But, continuing to assume that individualistic trade and international economic integration is the only respectable course, they assume that there necessarily must be something the West could have done, or can now do, that will save it from its plight, will make things work out for the best. The inadequacy of the remedies these searchers manage to come up with confirms the error of their diagnosis. In truth, international economic integration through unregulated international trade will have devastating effects on high-wage nations that are thrown into competition with equally efficient low-wage nations. The true answer is—that within the framework of free trade there is no answer.

For example, Robert B. Reich's influential book, *The Next American Frontier*, dramatically describes the great increase in international economic integration through trade in the past two decades, and the dominant role of cost differentials and of low wage rates in causing the shift of industries and jobs from the West to other nations. He sees that the only way (within an economically integrated world, which he takes for granted) that the West can maintain its existing standard of living is *to escape from this low-wage competition*. His proposal as to how this is to be done is stated thus:

> Skilled labor has become a key barrier against low-wage competition for the simple reason that is the only dimension of production in which these countries [the West] retain an advantage. Technological innovations may be bought or imitated by anyone. High-volume, standardized production facilities may be established anywhere. But production processes that depend on skilled labor must stay where that labor is.[12]

Restating this approach, Western are nations are doomed to a decline in their wage level and standard of living of monumental proportions unless they can avoid competition with the world's low-wage, overpopulated nations. To do this, the Western nations must find lines of production that cannot be moved to low-wage nations. The only such lines of production are those in which the Western workers can do things that low-wage foreign labor is unable to do. The author then goes on to argue that the Western nations will be able to shift into such noncompetitive lines of production, and paints a bright picture of what lies ahead, beyond "the next American Frontier." But the arguments and claims on which this view depends are of questionable realism.

What basis is there for asserting a general superiority of Western workers over Japanese workers, South Korean workers,

Taiwanese workers, Indian workers, Chinese workers? All nations include people of different personal abilities and training. The cultures and educational systems of societies affect the kinds of organizations their people can form and the accomplishments of which they are capable. But, as we have seen, the experience of recent decades has quite overturned the earlier-prevalent notion that American workers, say, were inherently superior to others, and this was the cause of their high wage rates. Recent discussion has noted that in some respects the workers of Japan and some other Asian nations are superior to Americans. Surely, there seems no basis now for asserting that Americans (or Westerners in general) have an inherent and permanent superiority over the people of other nations in production.

Thus it appears that there is no substantial volume of production activities that Westerners can perform that people of other nations potentially cannot perform as well. If this is true, the only possible fate of the West in a trade-integrated world is to share the world-wide, overpopulation-based, low standard of living. The only possible way of avoiding this fate is by avoiding international economic integration through trade. The basic tool for doing this is insisting on balance in internation trade, on terms that bring benefit to each nation.

What are the devices by which Reich proposes that the West shall escape from low-wage competition—the industries into which the West can move but low-wage nations cannot follow? He suggests "products like precision castings, specialty steel, special chemicals, process control devices, sensor devices, and luxury automobiles as well as . . . the design and manufacture of fiber-optic cable, fine ceramics, lasers, integrated circuits, and aircraft engines." The general formula is industries that "require precision engineering, complex testing, and sophisticated maintenance," that "are custom-tailored to the special needs of particular customers," or that "involve technologies that are changing rapidly." "These three product groups are relatively secure against low-wage competition because they depend on high-level skills rather than on standardized production."[13]

For the United States and the West to pin their hopes on this prescription would, it seems, be fatal. First, off-beat, small, and specialized industries do not provide any substantial number of jobs. Large numbers of people can be employed only in producing goods for which there is a large demand.

Second, only a small proportion of American workers are qualified for highly technical and demanding occupations. It will not be possible through training programs to tranform the great body of American workers into, as it were, industrial supermen, with capabilities not possessed by the workers of other nations.

Third, again, there seems no reason for believing that Americans (or Westerners) possess, or can acquire, a substantial superiority over Japanese, Chinese, Indians or other workers in the lines of work Reich recommends. With the organizational support of multinational corporations, the peoples of many low-wage nations are to be expected to provide low-income competition in these areas as well as others. It is necessary to give up the idea that there are fields in which the West has an *inherent* production superiority over low-wage nations.

Once attention is turned to realities such as the numbers of jobs in various lines of production and the actual abilities of of the people of different nations to perform them, the beguiling words in which Reich expresses his remedy lose their persuasive power. In a realistic frame of mind, one cannot believe in that "American frontier" beyond which the superior Americans avoid foreign competition by confining their unique skills to esoteric lines of production. This sounds rather too much like "the productivity of the American worker" in a new suit of clothes. And the stereotype of the "industrialized nations" and the "developing countries," the former presumably "advanced" and all-capable, the latter backward and consigned to performing simple and standardized production—this cannot be squared with present realities. In the circular reasoning of the orthodox analysis of "productivity," the people of poor nations had to be "unproductive" and incompetent—otherwise they would not be poor. Recent experience has shown the inadequacy of this stereotype, and has shown that people who are "poor" can quickly become formidable competitors of the high-wage workers of the West.

Similar doubts must be expressed as to the realism of the distinction between "standardized" and "nonstandardized" activities—the latter rewarding, the former unrewarding—and of the accuracy of the categories of "flexible-system industries" and "high-valued goods" as pointing the way to the West's escape from the devastating effects of competition with efficient, low-wage nations.

Reich is ahead of most observers in seeing that the economic problem of the West comes from the undercutting of Western economies by low-wage foreign competition. But his remedy cannot possibly save the West from that problem. The only remedy is for the West to decline to participate in general economic integration with the low-wage nations of an increasingly overcrowded world.

making American wages "competitive"

A quite different view as to the answer to the plight of the West is implicit in these statements:

> It would be nice to report that the difficult reductions in pay that many American workers have endured in the last couple of years have served to narrow the broad gap between U. S. and foreign pay levels, but that's simply not what has been happening.[14]

> The impression that U. S. labor has somehow emerged from the last recession leaner and more competitive doesn't hold up when placed in world-wide perspective. The best that can be said is that the U. S. position would look even worse if there hadn't been so many pay cuts and givebacks.[15]

In this interpretation, what is wanted is a reduction in U. S. wage rates to make them competitive with those of other nations. What is in question is not a *small* decline in American wage rates and standard of living. Figures on 1983 pay of production workers in manufacturing indicate that the decline in

U. S. wage rates to make them "competitive" in relation to West Germany would be 16 percent, for Sweden 27 percent, for Britain and Japan nearly 50 percent, and for Taiwan, Mexico, and South Korea nearly 90 percent.[16]

In the larger perspective of past discussion of this subject, the central point made by the orthodox economics has been that U. S. wage rates do not *need* to be competitive with foreign wage rates. That is the basic point of "the principle of comparative advantage." Our commentators, thinking in terms of experience rather than economic theory, do not seem to believe that under the present rules of the game United States wage rates can stay far above those in other nations.

But the point of the contention of the orthodox economics that low foreign wage rates do not undercut the wages of a high-wage nation was this: If this is not true, then the workers (and general populace) of a high-wage nation would reasonably insist on avoiding international trade with low-wage nations. For what possible benefit can there be in international trade that has the effect of forcing a large decline in the nation's wage rate and standard of living?

Recent statements that take for granted a need for United States wage rates to become competitive with those in other countries are anomalous in this respect. The people involved have seen from experience that low foreign wage rates under unregulated international trade do undercut the wage rates of a high-income nations. But, taking free trade as an unquestioned principle, they do not draw from this observation the only reasonable conclusion, that it is thus foolish and self-destructive for a high-wage nation to enter into unregulated trade with low-wage nations.

The enthusiasm that seems to be displayed for the prospect of reducing American wage rates and the American standard of living to, say, one tenth of the present level, so that we can be "competitive" with Taiwan (or by more than this, if India and China really get into this game)—this does seem to reflect a certain want of thought on the meaning of these events.

saved by the arrival of wonderland

The vision of "the next American frontier" of Reich is modest in relation to some other views of the impending transformation of the world—a transformation that is to be the economic salvation of the United States and the West. In this genre, we are offered a "postindustrial era" in which all the old, nitty-gritty problems are long forgotten, the decline of goods and the old-fashioned "smokestack industries" and the rise of "the service industries," the passage of "the mass economy" and its replacement by "the informative economy,"[17] and other such wonders—miracles, these, late-twentieth-century-style miracles.

Toward a Realistic Economics

The unrealism of the international-trade doctrines of the prevailing theoretical economics are illuminated by the confusions and delusions on the plight of the West to which it has given rise. Those who try to interpret recent events and future prospects on the basis of this version of economics can produce only delusions. The central causal factor in recent great shifts in industry and jobs, the undercutting of high-wage labor by low-wage labor, cannot be admitted to exist. The resulting explanations and remedies are rather like the diagnoses and prescriptions for malaria before the discovery of the microorganism that causes malaria—mythical stories in lieu of causal explanation.

The orthodox, natural-harmony, economics presents a basically unrealistic picture of economies and a potentially catastrophic guide to economic policy not because of any lack of ability or conscientiousness among its practitioners but because it reflects a false framework. The concepts and the view of the economy created by Adam Smith have commonly been extolled by economists as the of origin of "modern economics," or even of "scientific economics." It is more realistic to view the structure of this version of economics as designed to lend plausibility to the doctrines of natural-harmony individualism. In performing this function, it systematically misrepresents the actual workings of economies, and the actual effects of different sets of economic policies. The mechanical repetition in the recent economics literature of the centuries-old stereotypes of natural-harmony economics—quite as if nothing new or illuminating in international trade and the international shift of industries had happened in recent decades—conveys an important message about the character of professional economics. In this literature, "liberal trade" versus "protectionism" marches on, quite untouched by events.[18]

Why is it that the orthodox economics neglects evolutionary processes, does not explain the economic rise and fall of nations, basically misrepresents human behavior and human goals, neglects the role of population, the standard of living, and demand in order to depict economic welfare as depending only on mechanical processes of production, omits the complex interactions that characterize economies and orients itself to hypothetical, *ceteris paribus*, "optimal equilibrium positions," insists that in international trade cheap goods do not undersell dear goods, and low-wage labor does not take the jobs of high-wage labor?

Why does this economics depict "competition" as an inherently beneficent force? Why does it impute to people and firms knowledge and analytical abilities they obviously do not possess? Why does it so consistently reach the conclusion that—though no nonmiraculous explanation can be given of how this could happen—things automatically work out for the best when each person and firm myopically pursues its own interests. How is it that this economics so consistently supports the thesis that its creator designed it to support?

It seems clear that this doctrine is not science. It does not provide a description of the way the world works, but is a story that reflects a set of human preconceptions and wishes. The structure of this economics is not a set of discoveries about the world; it is the framework of a myth.

The treatment of international trade in the prevailing economic theory derived directly from its preconceptions. The policies of the United States and some other nations have been governed by this economic theory. On a central point, United States economic policy has been based on the belief that a high-wage nation like the United States cannot be damaged by unregulated, individualistic trade with low-wage nations—because of "the principle of comparative advantage." But "the principle of comparative advantage," as we have seen, is a fallacy, a sub-myth within the larger myth of *laissez-faire* economics. Such are the foundations of the economic future of the United States and the West.

The ongoing development of knowledge of evolutionary processes in living systems and societies provides a scientific framework for thinking about evolutionary processes of societal economic change. Within this framework, valid knowledge can be developed as the basis for guiding economic change in constructive directions, while leaving to individuals and firms that large scope for independent action that surely will characterize any effective and civilized economy.

The formulation of economics within the thought-world of modern science will provide cause-and-effect explanations of the diverse economic successes and failures of societies, and of the consequences of different kinds of economic policies under various circumstances. Such an economics could provide useful knowledge of the kind that has been so abundantly produced by some fields of scientific work.

As the foregoing chapters show, a modern, scientific economics presents a view of the effects of international trade that is very different from that of the prevailing individualistic economic theory. Unregulated trade by firms and individuals cannot be shown to be automatically beneficial to the nations involved. Quite the contrary, such unregulated trade across national boundaries is basically anomalous. It undermines essential capabilities of nations. It tends to spread overpopulation-caused poverty throughout the world. It undercuts the position of nations that achieve high incomes and high standards, the nations that would be in a position to serve as mankind's pathfinders to more advanced patterns of civilized life.

In the United States, the greatest impediment to realistic and responsible discussion of international trade is the continued dominance of an economics that propounds a set of fictions based on the eighteenth-century myth of natural harmony under individualism. The future of the West, and of all of mankind, depends on the early replacement of these misleading doctrines by a realistic economics within the framework of modern scientific thought.

7

Constructive Policies on International Trade

In economic affairs, the decades ahead must be a time of change and challenge, indeed, a time of "sink or swim." The economic world cannot stand still, and it cannot be made to correspond to the image presented by the prevailing economic theory and economics textbooks. The great structural changes in the pattern of international trade and international location of industry that have been set in motion will proceed according to their inexorable logic. Unless economic change is shifted to a new pattern, brought under intelligent control, the years ahead could bring cumulative economic deterioration and demoralization to the United States, the West, and to much of the world.

If realistic and purposeful policies can be followed, the degenerative processes that are under way can be halted, and events turned in a constructive direction. In seeking to do this, the first challenge is the intellectual one. The answer to the great economic problems of the time cannot be found within the now-dominant natural-harmony economics. The unrealism of this doctrine is the cause of the problem, and the major obstacle in the way of solving it. What is required now is to learn to think in realistic, scientific ways about matters that in the West have come to be viewed in terms of a set of misleading verbal formulas. A summary of some central ideas and a discussion of policy issues is given in this chapter.

International Trade; Some Basic but Unfamiliar Truths

As a basis for considering policy systems for international trade, it is useful to review some of the ideas that must underlie a realistic view of the subject. These ideas, of course, contrast with natural-harmony economics and other ideology-based approaches to the subject.

the effects of international trade on evolutionary processes are of dominating long-run importance

The pattern of international trade is an important feature of the structure of human affairs, a basic determinant of the direction taken by evolutionary change in the human situation. In particular, its role as a destructive factor could be a decisive one. Thus, the effect of the system of international trade that is of all-dominating importance in the long run is its influence on the direction of evolutionary change of the various nations, and of mankind. International trade can undermine the powers and capabilities of national governments, leaving mankind without a framework within which to guide affairs, meet challenges, and shape events to human purposes. International trade can economically integrate the peoples of the world into a structure that is incapable of self-control or self-guidance. One effect of this will be to cause the burdens of overpopulation to fall on all of mankind. Another effect is to enforce standards-lowering competition in economic affairs throughout the world.

But constructively guided international trade could contribute to favorable evolutionary change, providing gains from international specialization and intercourse while avoiding the degenerative processes that now threaten.

a pattern of international trade that benefits the nations involved must be an achievement of policy

No automatic mechanism makes international trade beneficial to the nations involved. The assurance of avoiding an outcome that is damaging to one or both nations can be provided only by realistically formed and effectively implemented policies of the national governments involved.

Among the reasons why it is impossible for a nation automatically to be benefitted by unregulated trade across national boundaries is that it is a matter of interpretation, of values and goals, what "benefits" a nation and what damages it. Another reason is that the important effects resulting from a pattern of international trade can be estimated only by the application of knowledge and analysis. The private party engaged for profit in trade across national boundaries does not have the incentive, the resources, or the viewpoint to analyze the broad effects of the pattern of trade to which he or she is contributing. In any case, private parties could not take effective actions to rectify a pattern of international trade that was damaging to one or more nations.

Thus, it is irrational to argue that international trade is automatically guided into beneficial channels as an unintended side effect of the self-seeking and myopic actions of firms and individuals. The justifications that traditionally have been given for this doctrine are fallacious. The required outcome can be achieved only through intelligent and informed actions of national governments.

international trade involves the hazard of three major kinds of destructive economic processes

Of the potential effects of a pattern of international trade, three major kinds of destructive processes merit special attention. First, international trade under modern conditions can cause an economic integration of nations that makes all peoples subject to overpopulation-caused poverty arising from high birth rates in any people and any area of the world. This economic integration brings into play an evolutionary structure in which no region can effectively defend its standard of living by limiting its own population. Thus, the arrangement would virtually guarantee world-wide overpopulation and poverty, and the loss of the positive features of human life that depend on a high standard of living.

Second, paralleling the degenerative competition among economically integrated nations in providing cheap labor through overpopulation, there would prevail a degenerative competition in achieving cheap production by cutting standards in worker protection, environmental protection, conservation of resources, and in other amenities and civilizing aspects of economic life.

Third, these and other kinds of anything-goes competition across national boundaries would lead to a competition among national governments to retain industries and jobs for their people. Being thrown into this kind of competition would deprive the national government of the power to guide its economy and protect the standard of living and the way of life of its people. In the same way that states in the United States are deprived of any effective ability to manage their economies by the free movement of goods, people, and funds between states, so in an economically integrated world nations would be stripped of the economic powers they have possessed in the past, and would be unable to serve as the major organizing unit for human economic life. Since there exists no higher-level organizing unit for human affairs, the outcome would be one tending toward anarchy in important aspects of human life.

in international trade, low wages undercut high wages

In international trade as in domestic trade, low costs undercut high costs and low wages undercut high wages. So also do cost-saving low production standards undercut high production standards. The conventional doctrine of economic theory that asserts the contrary, "the principle of comparative advantage," is an error.

Since wage levels and production standards commonly differ as between nations, individualistic trade across national boundaries generally causes a wage-lowering and standards-lowering competition. This tends to pull down the standard of living of high-income nations. It also tends to spread to other nations the burden of overpopulation generated by some societies or groups. Avoiding such lowest-common-denominator effects of international trade generally is accomplished by arrangements by which the trade between two nations is constrained to be in balance, and to be in balance on terms that bring benefits to both nations.

no natural process of "economic growth" will make all nations equally well off

A still-influential idea of the 1960s is that a "natural" or preprogrammed process of "economic growth" or "economic development" is working to make all nations well off, and ultimately to make them all equally affluent. If this were true, it would form an important part of the background against which international trade should be interpreted. The impending elevation of all nations to a uniformly high standard of living might seem to eliminate at least some of the hazards of unregulated international trade.

Unfortunately, this conception cannot be justified by experience, or reconciled with the ways of a cause-and-effect world. The past experience of nations exhibits no tendency toward automatic economic improvement, or toward equality of economic achievements of nations. In the recent past, as in earlier times, nations have generated a great diversity of economic performance, some striking successes, some near-total failures, and much variety of experience in between. The performances of various nations are explainable in terms of their circumstances and their policies, of the sets of causal factors operating in individual cases, and the cumulative processes in which these are involved. Some of the most appalling economic failures have been caused by unrealistic government policies, reflecting ideological formulas.

It is necessarily true, in the future as in the past, that the diverse causal factors operating in the different nations will cause them to exhibit a wide variety of economic performances. Policies toward international trade, and the economic integration it implies, are to be interpreted in relation to this kind of a world. Any assumption that a nation-equalizing "economic growth" now is transforming the world into a harmonious-trade area is unrealistic.

international trade and "rich nations helping poor nations"

A recently influential way of thinking about international trade is in terms of this set of ideas: "The level of incomes in different nations *ought* to be and naturally would be equal. But in actuality, some nations are 'rich' and others are 'poor.' This raises the question whether the rich nations did not get rich by exploiting the poor. In any case, the rich nations have an obligation to help the poor nations and to reduce or eliminate the *gap* between them. They also have an obligation to keep their markets entirely open to imports from the poor nations." Is this a realistic and reasonable way to think about the economic relations between nations, and about international trade? If not, why not?

It is not a realistic and resonable approach, for several reasons. First, it is not true that there is any natural tendency for nations to have equal incomes, nor any basis for presuming that a nation with a high level of income achieved it by taking from low-income nations. The wide differences in the circumstances, the histories, the population situations, and the institutions and policies of nations necessarily cause them to turn in quite different kinds of performances, and to experience different levels of income. That the economy of Japan is thriving while that of Burma is in a bad way reflects the policies and the circumstances of the nations, not a trick of fate, and surely not that the Japanese success is based on the Burmese failure. Thus, it is misleading to refer to these nations as "rich" and "poor," for these words in this usage imply that the differences in outcome are a matter of accident, or of blind chance—or of the "rich" being "rich" because they stole from the "poor." Calling them "high-income" and "low-income" nations avoids these misleading implications.

If the differences in the income levels of nations reflected luck or fate, it might be reasonable to agree to "share the luck," to take from the "rich" and give to the "poor." At least, this would do no great harm. But great harm can be done by an arrangement that appropriates the rewards accruing to effective economies and bestows them on ineffective economies. This permits the ineffective economies to persist in the policies that make them ineffective, and prevents the effective economies from providing the demonstration-effects that could lead other nations in a constructive direction.

It is misleading, also, to say that some nations must "help" others. In such matters, it is a matter of judgment—and often, in effect, of ideology—what will actually *help* a nation and what will damage it. Those who have emphasized the conception of "helping" have commonly defined "help" in a ritualistic way. Certain actions are *assumed* to help—and these are actions that fit in with the viewpoint, or even with the interests—of the "helper." Thus, some low-income nations that had little power to resist have been "helped" into ruination by symbolic programs of "assistance" that multiplied their populations or "modernized" them out of their old ways without providing them any viable new pattern of life.

The vocabulary of "helping" implies that actions arising from good motives are necessarily beneficial, and that the motives of the "helpers" are unquestionably good. The first proposition is surely wrong, and the second one is to be questioned. The effects of actions depend on cause-and-effect relations, not on motives. And "helpers" may be motivated more by their own need for feelings of superiority or power than by a real concern for the fates of those being "helped." Indeed, the preoccupation with symbolic forms of "help" and disregard for the actual effects of actions that so characterizes this approach implies that such is the case.

That it is desirable for nations, as for people, to do what can be done for those hit by misfortune would be widely con-

But a realistic and honest interpretation commonly discloses difficulties in determining what will help and what will damage, and often discloses that what really is needed is a change in behavior, rather than a gift that will confirm the behavior that is causing the problem.

It might seem reasonable to assert that "poor" nations have a *right* of free access to the markets of the "rich" nations. But these words present a false picture of the implications of such a set of arrangements. As was shown in earlier chapters, free access to a nation's markets is a blank check to undermine the standard of living of a high-income nation. Indeed, granting a "right" of low-income nations to sell freely in the markets of high-income nations could condemn all nations to overpopulation-caused poverty.

Realistic consideration of international economic relations and international trade thus cannot be conducted within the vocabulary of "rich" nations, "poor" nations, and "helping." This vocabulary is designed for the presentation of a particular kind of imaginary world. What is needed is to escape from imaginary worlds and face the outcomes that actually will result from different actions and policies.

mankind does not "stand or fall" as one unit

One frequently sees taken for granted that mankind as a whole stands or falls together, that the United States cannot prosper while Tanzania is in want, or that France cannot prosper while the United States is in difficulties. This view implies that efforts at economic improvement must be oriented to the condition of mankind as a whole, to the whole world, rather than to individual nations and national economies. Indeed, within this viewpoint an emphasis on the welfare of a specific nation may seem objectionably narrow-minded or old-fashioned.

Despite its emotional appeal, this doctrine is not consistent with experience. In truth, the rise of Ancient Rome was in no way influenced by what was going on in China. The meteoric rise of the Netherlands was in no way dependent on the situation in Japan or Madagascar, or the "undeveloped" state of most of the world. Indeed, if it were a rule of nature that no society could rise high while others remained low, the condition of mankind would have been hopeless, for there always have been societies living at the lowest level imaginable.

This will be no less true in the future. If the ability of the United States and the West to live at a high level were contingent on their somehow bringing about the same high economic level for Bangaladesh, Iran, China, and the Soviet Union, their position would be hopeless.

In fact, there is no general, mystical dependence of each society on all others, no need for them to experience "solidarity," to share the same fate, to cooperate, or even to have anything to do with one another. In some cases, a high degree of insulation of societies best serves their interests. Among living systems, including human societies, evolutionary success depends on multiple trials in the trial-and-error search for adaptive success and survival. The existence of multiple trials requires enough insulation of the operating units so that each can be a coherent, organized, potentially viable experiment. From an evolutionary viewpoint, thus, what is to be preferred is only limited contacts between societies. World-wide "solidarity" and "cooperation" virtually ensures evolutionary failure. Experience shows that most successful societies have been those that have achieved an unusual degree of internal coherence and problem-solving ability—as is true of firms and other organizations. For a society to lose these qualities and become closely enmeshed with others is ordinarily a ticket to declining performance.

The future of mankind is not damaged by the fact that some societies fail. An absence of failures would be dangerous, implying a lack of experimentation and diversification. Mankind's future depends not on the failures but on the successes. What is important for the long run is to generate some successes, as many, in as many different patterns and varieties, as possible, and to set up a framework within which it is the patterns of success that spread, are copied, come to prevail, rather than the failure-causing patterns.

These constructive evolutionary processes would be precluded by one-world economic integration. So it is reasonable to focus on success-causing patterns of national societies, and on a system of international economic relations within which these will be the patterns that prevail, within which the direction of change will be one that improves the lot of mankind.

international trade must include an element of "if we win, you lose"

The orthodox economics has asserted that international trade necessarily benefits both nations, and economists have heaped scorn on anyone who denied this. In truth, international economic relations necessarily involve elements of rivalry, or "for you to win means that we must lose"—as do all kinds of economic activities. This element in the picture must be recognized if the whole picture is to be viewed realistically.

International economic relations are rivalrous in at least two kinds of ways. First, the economic success or failure of a nation necessarily is judged in relation to the positions of other nations. If England were the most affluent nation in the world, people would not complain that it was "poor" because it failed to meet some absolute standard. If France were number two economically and England number one, then a failure by England would make France number one. In an important sense, this would make France better off, even though in absolute terms its standard of living had not risen.

The orthodox economics is consistently misleading in its denial of the role of relative or comparative standards in economic affairs. The "economic man" (and, presumably, the "economic nation") does not compare his position with those of other people. He does not notice whether he is the wealthiest or the most impoverished person in the city. His "utility" or "happiness" depends only on what volume of his in-built "economic wants" are being satisfied. Anyone can see that this is not the way people are, or nations are. Indeed, since built-in "economic wants" could not exist, that is not a way people *could be*.

The second kind of rivalrous element in international economic relations involves events that necessarily make one nation better off and another nation worse off. Say, the United States and Japan are in contention for dominance of the attractive computers industry. For either nation to win implies that the other one loses. In a somewhat different kind of case, the opening of trade between a high-wage and an equally efficient low-wage nation causes a shift of industries and jobs from the high-wage nation to the low-wage nation. The gain of the low-wage nation is at the same time the loss of the high-wage nation.

But while it distorts reality to deny the existence of such rivalrous relations in international economic dealings, it also would distort reality to assert that there is *nothing but* such rivalrous relations in international trade. Surely, mutually beneficial deals between nations can be arranged—though they may seldom result from individualistic trade. And a nation that in the short run loses by the shift of an attractive industry to another nation could, in some cases, gain in the long run in indirect ways. It also is true that some patterns of international trade could in the long run make mankind in general worse off, by bringing about universal poverty and overpopulation. To insist on any "principle" that denies this diversity of evolutionary processes and relations among nations prevents realistic interpretation of international trade.

firms and individuals have no natural right to engage in unregulated international dealings

It sometimes is argued, or taken for granted, that the "freedom" of people and firms would be unduly infringed by government regulation of international trade and the international movement of funds. This does not seem a reasonable position to take.

The income that a person acquires by investing, working, or establishing a business in the United States is not a strictly individual achievement. Engaging in the same activities in the Soviet Union, or Bangladesh or in Ethiopia would not have brought the same rewards. The income received reflects the characteristics of the United States economy, the contributions of others, the merits of the system, as well as the input of the individual involved. The income, thus, is not *his* or *hers* in any absolute sense. For the nation to impose regulations on what can be done with such income, and the terms on which it can be removed from the nation, is not unreasonable. The fact that such regulations are difficult to enforce does not imply that they are unreasonable or unnecessary, though it is a factor to be taken into account in designing actual policies.

Adam Smith and David Ricardo in creating the doctrine of "free trade" did not hold that "natural liberty" extended so far as to imply a "right" for people to engage in unregulated international dealings. In Adam Smith's interpretation, capitalism was justified because the capitalists were thrifty, saved their incomes, and invested them to the nation's benefit. But we recall that to justify unregulated international trade within this framework Smith had to assert that Nature had implanted in capitalists an instinct to invest at home rather than abroad. Smith's doctrine implies, thus, that if, in fact, capitalists take savings created in the United States economy and invest them in other countries, this is not an acceptable arrangement. It does not protect the interests of the United States.

If capitalists characteristically take the funds derived from the United States economy and shift them to other countries—the argument might be expanded—they are in a sense appropriating to their personal benefit something that is an achievement of the United States society. In such a case, the rest of the society would have a strong incentive to arrange to undertake the society's investment through "socialism," and keep the rewards of the society's achievements for further investment at home. For a person thus to appropriate some of the social achievement of the nation, it might be said, is rather like an official in a corporation appropriating to himself some of the property of the corporation by selling its trade secrets or its property.

The idea that people have an inherent right to engage in unregulated international transactions is unrealistic also because of its inconsistency with powers and capabilities of governments that are taken for granted, and that, on consideration, are essential to the success of the nation. How many nations now are ready to give up the ability to have an economic policy for their nation, to determine their own rules on environmental protection and worker protection? How many accept the proposition that enforcing a narrow framework of basic laws is all they are permitted to do? It is inconsistent to assert a "right" of people to unregulated international transactions in the present-day world, while pretending that governments continue to exercise their accustomed and essential powers.

Dealing with Standards-Lowering Competition in International Trade

Among the potential problems that must be dealt with by reasonable arrangements for trade across national boundaries is the tendency toward degenerative competition in production standards. A nation that requires standards in the work-place that protect the health and safety of employees thereby imposes on its producers costs that do not have to be incurred by firms producing in nations that do not enforce such standards. Under these conditions, competition among them will tend to force firms to shift production from high-standards nations to low-standards nations. This may be accomplished in part by the firms of high-standards nations failing and being replaced by those of low-standards nations. The same kind of problem applies to all kinds of cost-affecting standards: standards in environmental protection, in resource conservation, in the preservation of historical treasures and aesthetic values.

The competition imposed upon firms under unregulated international trade will tend to lower such standards without limit. The movement of industries and jobs from high-standards to low-standards nations will cause a competition among nations to retain industries and jobs by lowering their standards. The effect will be not only to prevent nations' imposing standards that are unreasonably high, but to prevent them from maintaining any standards at all. The force of competition is to require firms to avoid all costs that can be avoided. Such competition includes no in-built mechanism that distinguishes reasonable from unreasonable regulations and standards. If this ingredient is to be supplied, it must come from national governments.

In seeking arrangements for international trade that would avoid standards-lowering competition without damaging the interests of any particular nation, what kind of approach is to be considered? One response is to suggest that the standards of the high-standards nations should be imposed on all nations, or on all nations producing for export. The economic integration imposed by international trade then would lead to a standards-raising structure rather than to standards-lowering competition.

But this approach does not seem reasonable or feasible for general application, though it might work for trade between some similarly situated nations. The production standards that it is reasonable for nations to impose depend on their economic circumstances, their standards of living, their abilities to design regulations and to enforce them. The standards that would be reasonable for a high-income nation might be an unattainable "luxury" for a nation that suffered chronic unemployment and economic want. The limited ability of some nations to define and enforce such standards must be taken into account. Also, what standards are reasonable and desirable is to some extent a matter of judgment, of taste, of values. Unanimity among societies on such matters is not likely to be attainable, or necessarily desirable. Thus, the universal enforcement of the "highest standards" in production—though it may seem an attractive "principle"—is not a feasible or reasonable course of action.

To the workers and owners in an industry in a high-standards nation, it understandably would seem to be "unfair competition" for their production and their jobs to be undersold by goods on the basis of cost-saving from production in a low-standards nation. From their limited perspective, it would seem that equal standards—or some compensating penalty on low-standards producers—would be required to prevent such "unfair competition." But to follow this approach would violate the conception that differences in production standards among nations may be reasonable or necessary because of the differences in their circumstances. What is wanted, it seems, is an arrangement that will permit nations to have different production standards, while preventing this condition from leading to standards-lowering competition among firms and among nations or from standing in the way of mutually beneficial trade between nations.

To a degree, this problem would be solved by general arrangements by which nations arrange for the trade between them to be in balance. If the trade between two nations is kept in balance through such a mechanism, this precludes a one-sided shift of industries from the high-standards nation to the low-standards nation. Access to the markets of the high-standards nation would depend on the criteria that are being applied by the governments in arranging balanced trade. But three additional kinds of difficulties need to be kept in mind.

First, even though low-standards Country L is prevented from a general undercutting of the production of high-standards Country H in its home market by the negotiation of balanced trade by Countries L and H, this does not prevent L from using its advantage to undercut the sales of H in other nations, and thus taking over its export markets. This action, then, pressures Country H to cut its production standards.

The basis for dealing with this competition-in-third-countries problem perhaps lies in the general negotiation of packages of balanced trade between nations. Say that in Nation T the products formerly imported from the high-standards nation, H, now are potentially undersold by those from Country L because of the cost advantage of its low-standards production. Under free trade, this situation commonly would involve unbalanced trade between T and L, which would be disadvantageous to T. Under an arrangement of negotiated, balanced trade packages, Countries H and L will compete not only in terms of their ability to provide imports cheaply to Country T, but also in their ability to absorb the kinds of goods it wishes to export. This creates, as it were, a different kind of ball game. As was noted in Chapter 6, free trade is a biased arrangement that rewards selling cheap but does not reward having a large market for advanced goods. Trade packages negotiated between nations would be free of this bias.

A second difficulty associated with national differences in production standards is this. It is agreed that it may be reasonable for Country H, say, to let its domestic steel industry be undercut by imports from Country L that are cheap because Country-L firms are not required to protect the safety of their workers or to protect the environment. Such an action need not damage the interests of Country *H*. These interests must be judged in terms of the whole trade package between the countries. No single element in the package can be evaluated in isolation.

But may there not be a moral problem in that by buying goods produced under these conditions Country H is making itself a party, say, to "crimes" against the steel workers of Country L, and against its environment and its future? This is an awkward question. Lying behind it is the issue of the validity of the government of Country L. If the government has unquestioned validity and its policies assuredly represent the values and the goals of Country L, then perhaps it is not for Country H to presume to intrude. But if the government is of questionable validity—which perhaps most governments are, in some degree—then the issue is raised whether Country H is not acting in league with an invalid government of Country L in actions that are grievously damaging to its people, and perhaps contrary to what might be viewed as minimum standards of civilized behavior. It is important to raise here this kind of question but, fortunately, not essential to our present purposes to pretend to offer a practical answer to it.

A third implication of national differences in production standards is this: Low production costs based on low standards might give a nation some advantage in negotiations with other nations in gaining desirable industries. This would provide a basis for standards-lowering competition among nations. Only by competing with other nations at the lowering of production standards could a nation hope to retain the industries and lines of production that would permit it to have a favorable economic future.

Negotiation of balanced trade packages among nations would remove the bias or asymmetry of the free-trade rules and put large, high-income and high-standards nations in a position better to protect themselves against cost-cutting competition. But this would not fully deal with the difficulty. Consider the position of a small, medium-income nation that tries to maintain high production standards. It would be in a weaker position to hold attractive industries than would a similarly situated low-standards nation.

It thus remains true that without some additional rules for international trade a nation that can undercut the production costs of other nations because of low production standards gains thereby an advantage in attracting the rewarding industries. This factor tends to cause standards-cutting competition among nations. This is one of the factors that would need to be kept in mind in considering the rules for any system of international trade.

Preserving the Nation as the Essential Organizing Entity for Civilized Society

Human beings exist only as social beings, in organized groups. Their great civilizations arose from episodes in which people's intellectual and social potential was developed by an unusually effective societal framework. The routine achievements on which present-day life depends come from people working in structured organizations, business firms, government agencies, research organizations—which keep the autos rolling off the assembly lines, the airplanes flying, the fertilizers, insecticides, medicines flowing to sustain the existing pattern of life.

It is logically anomalous—though perhaps psychologically understandable—that in an era of such achievements of human organizations and such dependence of the existing way of life on complex, functional organizations there rises to dominance the myth of the inner-guided, self-sufficient human individual, and the doctrine that things automatically work out for the best when each person does as he or she wishes. The rise in recent decades of individualistic economics has been a major basis for the rise of these beliefs—which are so in conflict with the realities of the existing situation.

The top-level organization that provides the framework within which all of these other organizations can develop and function is the nation. The increasing complexity of production and of economic organizations, the intricacy of the interrelations among them, and the rapidity of change in the modern world create increasing needs for and demands on the nation as the framework-setter for human activities.

Under present-day conditions, one essential role of the nation is protecting the society—particularly the advanced, high-income society—from overpopulation, damaging immigration, the wage-lowering effects of unbalanced international trade, and standards-lowering effects of international economic dealings. The national government cannot perform these functions unless it possesses the necessary powers and ability to act on behalf of the nation. And it will lose these powers if it is thrown into competition with other governments to retain industry and jobs. This will happen if nations confer on individuals and firms excessive powers to engage in international transactions detrimental to the interests of the nation.

The national government cannot protect the standard of living of the society if it cannot limit immigration, or prevent the same wage-lowering effects from being caused by the blank-check importing of goods. It cannot protect the society's standards in worker protection, environmental protection, resource conservation, product safety unless it can protect its firms from an inflow of goods produced under standards-cutting conditions in other countries. It cannot protect the stability of the nation's economy unless it can limit the international skipping of industries and hot-money movements among nations.

An important requirement of the arrangements for international economic dealings, thus, is that they must reserve to nations the powers and capabilities that are essential for their orderly and constructive guidance of national economies, and their performance of other essential functions, powers and capabilities that in the present-day world can be exercised by no other entity but the national government.

Ways of Managing Trade Between Nations

Once it is recognized that trade that is mutually beneficial to the nations involved cannot possibly result from unregulated dealings across national boundaries by firms and individuals, it is natural to turn to the one arrangement that actually is capable of bringing about such mutually beneficial trade. That is the management of internation trade by negotiated trade agreements among governments. It is for the governments to bring about the condition that trade, say, between "England" and "Portugal" actually be beneficial to both England and Portugal.

Though explicit and comprehensive trade deals between governments have been largely limited to the centrally planned economies, many governments have guided their international trade in one way or another. Governments have placed barriers in the way of imports thought to be detrimental to the nation's interests, because of the character of the imports and the industry they represented, the rapid growth of the imports, or the general excess of the nation's imports. Direct negotiations between governments over trade have occurred in cases like the agreement between the United States government and the government of Japan through which a quota was imposed on sales of Japanese automobiles in the United States.

An arrangement that involves the explicit balancing of trade and the exacting of a *quid pro quo* by the importing nation is "countertrade," or "offset" arrangements. These were estimated in 1984 to apply to about eight percent of the world's merchandise trade, and to be increasing in importance in recent years.[1] Such arrangements ordinarily involve agreements not between governments but between the government of the importing nation, or firms of that nation acting under its policies, and the foreign firm making the sale. The foreign exporting firm agrees to buy some quantity of goods from the importing nation, under a "counter-purchase arrangement" or to buy or accept in payment goods based on the original transaction, such as finished goods made with the equipment it sold in the original transaction, termed a "buy-back" arrangement.[2]

Such arrangements can have constructive effects in permitting a nation to avoid or limit unbalanced imports in a way that does not deal a "sledgehammer" blow to trade in general. That is, the arrangement is one kind of application to trade across national boundaries of the practice of mutuality or reciprocity. But this is an unbalanced arrangement in pitting a national government, on one side, against competing firms on the other side. The nation that does not engage in such practices will tend to be placed at a disadvantage in relation to those that do. This will be true in a special sense if the nation using offset or countertrade arrangements does so as a means of gaining for itself, at the expense of another nation, industries that will be rewarding in the future.[3]

Arrangements for trade that are negotiated directly between the two governments involved thus would be more balanced, would, as it were, put the cards on the table, and would open up the potential for kinds of mutually advantageous trade deals that could not be worked out at lower levels but require the larger perspective and powers of the national governments. The positive side of such arrangements is that they would open the way to mutually profitable arrangements for international trade and international economic specialization that are not feasible now because the only agency with the breadth of viewpoint and authority to make them is the national government. The decisions that have to be made are decisions involving the interests of nations. Despite the rhetoric about "competition" and "the free market," firms cannot act effectively or responsibly on behalf of a nation.

For national governments to oversee and guide international trade through such arrangements with other governments would not require an extension of central planning of production, or the nationalization of industries. The production of goods could be left as much as desired in the hands of private firms. The needed limitation or guidance of trade could be achieved through requiring licenses for certain kinds of transactions—as is done now in special cases. The licenses would be issued by the government in the required volume and under the required side-conditions to private firms. Even in cases in which governments made direct contracts with one another for the delivery of specified goods, the actual operations could be carried out by private firms acting under contracts with the governments. Perhaps in many cases trade could be permitted to proceed without such arrangements, and only kept under surveilance by governments to assure that it does not expand or change in form in a way that is inconsistent with the over-all program of mutually advantageous trade between the nations involved.

Surely such management of international trade by national governments could involve many kinds of problems. Differences among governments in competence could seriously affect the outcome. Some governments would find it difficult to create an agency that could act knowledgeably and intelligently on behalf of the nation in trade matters.

There is a hazard that nations that are in a strong position because of their size, their lack of dependence on international trade, or their possession of something that other nations badly need would take advantage of nations that are in a weak bargaining position. Some nations might make trade agreements and not live up to them. For some nations, the government's assumption of a role in guiding international trade could seriously increase the burdens imposed by a poorly organized, red-tape-bound, or corrupt government bureaucracy. The new regulations could become the basis for new kinds of graft and bribery of government officials.

All such potential difficulties need to be taken seriously. But the fact that managing international trade involves difficulties and inconveniences does not imply that managing international trade is not necessary. Dealing with a heart ailment involves difficulties and inconveniences, but the fact that it is difficult does not imply that it is superfluous. Management by governments of trade between nations can prevent patterns of trade that are seriously disadvantageous to nations, even ruinous to them. This is a requirement that must be met. There seems to be no other way of meeting it.

Potentialities for Multi-Nation Trade Arrangements

It is often cited as a positive feature of unregulated international trade that it can construct multilaterial patterns of trade: United States sells machinery to Venezuela, which sells oil to Japan, which sells automobiles to the United States. In economic theory, all of this balances out nicely and has no indirect effects, but we are aware that the reality is very different from the theory.

Can trade regulated and guided by national governments generate patterns of three-way trade, or more complex patterns of trade? Or does the existence of such national guidance of trade force it into a strictly bilateral framework?

Clearly, it is feasible for trade packages to be arranged by more than two nations. Where there exists a potential for a set of nations to gain from a trade package of this type, their governments will have an incentive to work out the necessary arrangements. The ability to keep the trade under control, in accordance with a plan, and to make larger and longer commitments than would be feasible for firms, may permit the working out of some constructive patterns of trade that could not have been developed under individualistic trade.

The systems of contractual arrangements among firms on which the ordinary operations of economies are based are extremely complex. The development of such intricate patterns of dealings depends on the use of explicit contracts among firms. Such contractual arrangements bring to the system of activities the order, predictability, and controllability that make possible the planning of elaborate sets of dealings that are mutually advantageous to the firms involved. If firms could not operate through such contracts and had to flounder along on the basis of week-to-week dealings, they could not arrange such complex patterns of mutually advantageous specialization.

Trade contracts or formal trade agreements among nations would involve the extension to a higher organizational level of the planning and guidance instrument through which firms achieve the wonders of modern production. In an economic world that is based on mutually advantageous contractual arrangements among firms, it is anomalous that mutually advantageous contractual arrangements among nations are not made—and that contracts between firms are assumed to be a substitute for contracts between nations. Correcting this anomaly should make possible new kinds of benefits from international trade—as well as protecting nations against the great hazards of unregulated trade.

Realism and the Rescue of the West

Perhaps most of the great failures and collapses of societies have reflected unrealism. Few could not have been prevented or mitigated by a combination of realistic thought and effective organization. The unrealistic beliefs that caused such human tragedies were not random perturbations of the mind, or reflections of simple ignorance. They arose from unrealistic theories and ideas, which in most cases flattered people or served the psychological or material interests of a group.

After the Second World War, the potential for economic integration among the nations of the world radically increased. There also occurred a "population explosion" that has more than doubled the world's population since the Second World War, adding some two billion persons to an already-crowded planet. Another event of this period was a great human achievement, the rapid transformation of their economy by the Japanese and their abrupt surpassing in many ways of the United States and the West, which for so long had been at the top of the economic pyramid. A number of other Asian nations copied or approximated the Japanese achievement.

What were the implications of these events? What policies were needed to assure that the resulting processes of change went in a constructive direction? Unfortunately, this question was hardly asked. The economists, mankind's supposed experts on the subject, were the main impediment to the realistic analysis of the situation and its implications. They continued to propound their ancient fallacies: natural harmony makes economic activities self-regulating under economic individualism; self-seeking dealings across national boundaries by individuals and firms—labelled "free trade"—are automatically beneficial to the nations involved; low wage rates undercut high wage rates within a nation but have no such effect in international trade.

It is the dominance of these false doctrines that explains the present economic plight of the United States and the West. Had people not been blinded by these prestige-laden falsehoods, they could hardly have failed to see that Japaese goods, and Taiwanese and South Korean goods, displaced American-made goods because they were cheaper, and that they were cheaper because they were produced by workers earning wage rates that were only a fraction of American wage rates. And ordinary common sense sufficed to infer that continuation of the shift of industries, jobs, and production to low-wage nations would have serious, if not catastrophic, effects on the West. It then could have been obvious that preventing such an economic debacle required some arrangement to balance the trade between nations, so that industries and jobs would not shift from high-wage to low-wage nations.

Such arranging of balanced trade was what was necessary to prevent the continued loss of industries and jobs by high-wage nations, and to prevent the general degenerative process by which high wage rates and high standards of living anywhere in the world are pulled down to a lowest-common-denominator level, a level that the population explosion guarantees will be a very low level. Such arranging of balanced trade between nations was necessary also to make such trade fit the general pattern of constructive economic dealings and exchange—that it be carried out in such a way that both parties benefit, not so that one party to the trade is ruined—and when indirect effects are taken into account perhaps people generally are damaged. All of this is common sense. But what ruled the policies of the West was not common sense, but "economic theory."

Interpretations of events based on this economic theory could only lead to errors, or myths. For example, those who held to the idea that international trade could not be damaging to a nation had to argue that the loss of jobs and industries by the West could not have been caused by free trade. Thus it had to be explained in terms of something the West was doing wrong, some defect in its "productivity" or "efficiency." This led to fanciful explanations of what happened to the "productivity," and how to get it back again.

It is not difficult to imagine the United States and the West in the years ahead playing out a script that derives from the unrealistic doctrines of economic theory. Many economists wear blinders that will induce them to continue their crusade against "protectionism" all the way to the sinking of the West. Others would have the West adopt a futile "industrial policy" that tries to keep afloat through subsidies industries that are being radically undersold by the products of low-wage, efficient foreign industry.

And there is the script in which the West escapes from low-wage foreign competition by shifting its hundreds of millions of workers into off-beat or esoteric lines of production, on the notion that in these activities—unlike the basic and large-employment industries—Westerners have an inherent superiority over other peoples, and thus can escape their low-wage competition. There is also the approach of waiting to be rescued by the imminent arrival of the new era, by the passing of a new frontier—by an epochal event in which Nature shows that it not only designed the world for human benefit but, more specifically, planned a miraculous last-minute rescue of the West.

Will the United States and the West escape from such delusions, come to interpret international trade realistically, and respond intelligently to the situation that actually exists? This question is *decisive* for the future of the West. It is not to be expected that the fictions of economic theory will lead to policies that will save the West from the process of deterioration in which it is now engaged. A successful recovery can be caused only by realism.

Notes

Chapter 1 International Trade in Today's World

1. On the way evolution works, its implications, and the great resistance that has been demonstrated to accepting evolutionary explanations of events, see Garrett Hardin, *Nature and Man's Fate* (New York: New American Library, 1959). Contributions to the formulation of economics with reference to evolutionary processes are David Hamilton, *Evolutionary Economics* (Albuquerque: University of New Mexico Press, 1970) and Kenneth E. Boulding, *Evolutionary Economics*, (Beverly Hills, Calif.: Sage Publications, 1981).

2. An excellent brief interpretation, with references, is given in Peter T. Manicas and Paul F. Secord, "Implications for Psychology of the New Philosophy of Science," *American Psychologist*, 38 (April 1983), pp. 399–413. Major contributions to the field are Roy Bhaskar, *A Realist Theory of Science* (Atlantic Highlands, N.J.: Humanities Press, 1978); and R. Harré and E. H. Madden, *Causal Powers* (Totawa N.J.: Rowan and Littlefield, 1975).

3. The great, recent breakthrough in understanding of the role of territorial groups in evolutionary processes was provided by V. C. Wynne-Edwards, *Animal Dispersion in Relation to Social Behavior* (New York: Hafner Publishing Company, 1962). A survey of recent contributions and controversies is provided by Richard F. Johnston, ed., *Annual Review of Ecology and Systematics* (Palo Alto, Calif.: Annual Reviews Inc., 1983), an annual publication. Useful background knowledge is provided in Lester J. Bilsky, ed. *Historical Ecology; Essays on Environment and Social Change* (Port Washington, N.Y.: Kennikat Press, 1980).

4. An illustrative collection, with references, is Ervin Laszlo, *Introduction to Systems Philosophy* (New York: Harper and Row, 1972).

5. For a general discussion of the approach and references, see V. L. Parsegian, *This Cybernetic World of Men, Machines, and Earth Sys-*

tems (Garden City, N.Y.: Doubleday and Company, 1973). An early but broad discussion is given in Stafford Beer, *Decision and Control* (New York: John Wiley and Sons, 1966).

6. Illustrative contributions are Richard Day and A. Cigno, *Modelling Economic Change; The Recursive Programming Approach* (Amsterdam: North-Holland, 1978); T. H. Naylor, *Computer Simulation Experiments with Models of Economic Systems* (New York: John Wiley and Sons, 1971); and Richard R. Nelson and Sidney G. Winter, *An Evolutionary Theory of Economic Change* (Cambridge, Mass.: Harvard University Press, 1983).

7. Smith's argument that international trade is automatically beneficial to the nations involved is given in *The Wealth of Nations* (New York: Random House, 1937, first published in 1776), pp. 421–424. It is in this passage that he uses his wonderfully suggestive metaphor of the "invisible hand" working to make things work out for the best for mankind.

8. Guy Routh, *The Origin of Economic Ideas* (New York: Random House, 1975), p. 27. Also relevant is his observation: "And the fact that . . . the main corpus of theory ante-dates the industrial revolution by a hundred years and lives on in the textbooks of today is, indeed, a testimony that it is remote enough from reality to be impervious to those substantial changes, for better or worse, to which reality has been a prey" (p. 104). Routh sees Adam Smith as only the popularizer of natural-harmony economics, the major creator of which was Sir William Petty, writing a hundred years earlier.

Chapter 2 Basic Ideas on International Trade

1. On this subject, see Garrett Hardin, *Nature and Man's Fate* (New York: New American Library, 1959) and G. Ledyard Stebbings, *Darwin to DNA, Molecules to Humanity* (San Francisco: W. H. Freeman and Company, 1982). A readable and interesting source on current work is the articles in *Natural History*, particularly the articles on evolution by Stephen Jay Gould.

2. The role of localized or territorial groups in evolution, and the related points of (1) the social or group-based element in species behavior and survival in man and some other species and (2) the multilevel character of evolutionary processes were developed in the basic contribution to the understanding of evolution of V. C. Wynne-Edwards, *Animal Dispersion in Relation to Social Behavior* (New York: Hafner Publishing Company, 1962).

3. Friedrich List especially emphasized and understood that the orthodox economics stemming from Adam Smith rested on the unrealistic conception of a world of individuals, in which nations played no substantial role. This imaginary world was beneficently guided by the actions of individuals. The situation represented "natural harmony," under "natural liberty," thus embodying Smith's ideology. List draws a basic distinction between his "political economy," or economics relating to the actual world in which nations exist and play an important organizing role in human affairs, and Adam Smith's, as List puts it, "cosmopolitical economy," which is formulated as if nations were of no significance—and ought to be of no significance. See Friedrich List, *The National System of Political Economy* (Fairfield, N.J.: Augustus M Kelley, 1977, a reprint of the 1885 edition), especially Chapter 11.

4. As do the recent orthodox economics and recent popular defenses of the free-trade doctrine, Smith presents a picture in which the only people who are not supporters of free trade are those who are motivated by a narrow, personal interest or viewpoint, or who are ill-informed on the subject. See *The Wealth of Nations* (New York: Random House, 1937), pp. 402–403. Smith gives a purported presentation and refutation of "the principle of the commercial or mercantile system," as he terms it, but his presentation does not do justice to the views of those he takes as his adversaries. A reasonable and balanced view of the subject, presented just nine years before Smith's book, James Steuart's, *An Inquiry into the Principles of Political Economy*, was ignored by Smith.

Chapter 3   Effects of International Trade

1. This evocative term was popularized by Barry Bluestone and Bennet Harrison, *The Deindustrialization of America* (New York: Basic Books, 1982). The interpretation of the causes of the problem and its potential cure given in that book differs from the one developed here.

2. Carlo M. Cipolla, *Before the Industrial Revolution; European Society and Economy, 1000–1700* (New York: W. W. Norton, 1976), pp. 240–244.

3. This is substantially the interpretation given by Cipolla, *ibid.*, pp. 242–243.

4. Those who believe that international trade is automatically beneficial to each nation, in effect, *deduce* from this proposition that if a nation loses an attractive industry through international trade it must necessarily gain an industry that is at least as advantageous—otherwise

the country would not have benefitted from the international trade—"but we *know* such a thing cannot be." The logic is valid; the premise is false.

In that period when the standard of living and the technology of the times made textile manufacture the *leading* industry of the times, the nation that lost this industry could not gain anything that would make up for its loss. Since at any time the leading industries are determined by tastes, technology, the world standard of living, and the production capabilities of different nations, it is in a certain sense true that when Nation A gains by taking over a leading industry, other nations must lose by giving it up. In the 1980s, if the United States loses its dominant position in computers, its loss cannot automatically cause the rise of some new, equally rewarding, industry that will recompense the United States for the loss.

5. The point is supported by the detailed accounts of the striking episodes of economic rise and decline of nations during this period that are given in the literature of economic history. Accounts that point up the issue are those of Cipolla, *op. cit.*, Chapter 10, and Friedrich List, *The National System of Political Economy* (Fairfield, N.J.: Augustus M. Kelley, 1977), pp. 3-115.

6. On this, see List, *op. cit.*, especially pp. 41-61.

7. Cipolla, *op. cit.*, p. 260.

8. Adam Smith, *The Wealth of Nations* (New York: Random House, 1937), especially pp. 67-74. Smith applied the prevailing view of this time in making the nation's population, and its tendency toward overpopulation, the dominating factor determining its wage rate and standard of living in the long run—though this pessimistic doctrine was quite inconsistent with the thesis of natural harmony under individualism, which he applied to international trade and some other major topics. After the mid-1800s, the orthodox or Smithian economics shifted toward bringing the population factor under the guidance of natural harmony, arguing that population is automatically self-regulating if "economic growth" is achieved, or if some other condition is met.

9. This discussion relates to nations that are internally economically integrated, are not divided into classes or regional groups that are insulated from one another. Where such internal integration does not prevail and a situation of noncompeting groups exists, a group within a nation may have some of the characteristics here associated with the nation. For example, an upper class that can maintain barriers to its economic integration with lower classes may be able within itself to

gain some of the advantages that are here associated with the high-income nation. The system of education that underlay the successes of England in the eighteenth and nineteenth centuries was largely an upper-class arrangement, depending on the incomes, the privileges, and the group-culture of the upper classes. Shifting among classes occurred, but only to a limited degree. Such nonintegration among classes or groups within a nation always exists to some extent, but in a degree and a particular form that differs widely among cases.

10. A suggestive report is "Raising the Ante; Competition by States to Lure Firms Turns Into a Fierce Struggle," *The Wall Street Journal*, December 28, 1983, p. 1.

The interpretation of this matter is complicated by the consideration that some of the regulations and taxes imposed on business by governments doubtless are harmful, and their removal is a benefit. But the point is that the competition among governments here in question does not work to remove unreasonable regulations and retain reasonable ones, but to eliminate the good with the bad. A kind of competition that pressures governments to remove unreasonable regulations and impose reasonable ones requires a quite different interaction-process, a different kind of "competition," and a different set of rules.

Chapter 4 The Harmonious-Trade Area, and International Trade

1. Adam Smith, *The Wealth of Nations* (New York: Random House, 1937), pp. 421–424. Smith asserts: "Every individual endeavours to employ his capital as near home as he can, and consequently as much as he can in the support of domestic industry" (p. 421). But the two conditions of being "near home" and being "domestic industry" rather than "foreign industry" are by no means equivalent.

David Ricardo shifted the argument a bit: "Experience . . . shews, that the fancied or real insecurity of capital, when not under the immediate control of its owner, together with the natural disinclination which every man has to quit the country of his birth and connexions, and intrust himself with all his habits fixed, to a strange government and new laws, checks the emigration of capital." *Principles of Political Economy and Taxation* (Harmondsworth, England: Penguin Books, 1971, first published in 1817), p. 155. In fact, British capital during the 1800s emigrated to India, the United States, and other places both remote and foreign in very large volume.

2. An illuminating area in which to seek examples of such careful design and revision of rules and thorough enforcement of them is

sports. In professional football, for example, the rules are subject to frequent adjustment by a knowledgeable and responsible committee, the purpose being improving the character of the game and correcting any unsatisfactory features of the game as it emerges from the existing rules. And elaborate arrangements are made to enforce the rules, with a team of officials on the field conspicuously engaged in minute-by-minute observation of the actions of players. It is unlikely that anyone who knew about the game would propose that all of this should be abolished, in the name of "deregulation."

3. Alexander Hamilton, *Report on Manufactures* (1791).

4. Friedrich List, *The National System of Political Economy* (Fairfield, N. J.: Augustus M. Kelley, 1977), e. g., Chap. 34.

Chapter 5   Patterns of International Trade

1. But in the modern world, in contrast to earlier times, we recall, such an economically backward nation can under some circumstances quickly begin to undercut an advanced nation by making use of its low wages and cost-saving low production standards, joined with the power of multinational corporations abruptly to transfer to it the fruits of the experience and achievements of the advanced nations.

2. A 1984 headline dramatizes the point: "Fast-Rising American Export: Jobs," *U. S. News and World Report*, Jan. 23, 1984, p. 12. The article reports on the shifting of production of computers, shoes, clothing, and automobiles to other countries to take advantage of low wages and tax breaks.

"Union leaders vow to stem the erosion of American payrolls. The United Auto Workers claimed that up to 25,000 U. S. and Canadian jobs will be lost to Ford's 500-million-dollar Mexican plant, where 130,000 small cars will be made each year starting in late 1986—mostly for export to the U. S. and Canada."

3. The *neutrality* of money, and of processes caused by change in the quantity of money, was a major theme of the orthodox economics. Adam Smith's application of this approach to banking and bank-created money underlies the perverse policies that led to subsequent episodes of severe inflation and depression. The view that bank-created money is neutral or self-regulating is the basis of "the commercial loan theory of banking" or "the real-bills doctrine." This was an element underlying Federal Reserve inaction in the great U. S. economic decline of 1929-1933.

"The principle of comparative advantage" is essentially an assertion of the neutrality of international trade, which is claimed to make each

Notes   233

nation better off, and to have no "side effects"—just as money is claimed to facilitate exchange, and to have no side effects. Such unjustifiable assertions of neutrality, denial of "side effects," and reliance on *ceteris paribus* to omit from the picture causal relations and processes that do not fit in with its ideology-based story appear to be essential characteristics of the orthodox, individualistic economics.

Chapter 6   Truths and Fictions about International Trade

1. Paul A. Samuelson, *Economics*, 11th ed. (New York: McGraw-Hill Book Company, 1980), pp. 627, 630.

2. Adam Smith, *The Wealth of Nations* (New York: Random House, 1937), pp. 421–424. Smith's classic passage runs: "By preferring the support of domestic to that of foreign industry, he intends only his own security; and by directing that industry in such manner as its produce may be of the greatest value, he intends only his own gain, and he is in this, as in many other cases, led by an invisible hand to promote an end which was no part of his intentions" (p. 423).

For David Ricardo's parallel treatment, see his *Principles of Political Economy and Taxation* (Harmondsworth, England: Penguin Books, 1971), pp. 152 ff. Ricardo explicitly says that trade across national boundaries works differently than other trade: "The same rule which regulates the relative value of commodities in one country, does not regulate the relative value of the commodities exchanged between two or more countries" (p. 152). It is significant here that Ricardo refers to the trade as *between two or more countries*, rather than as *between firms or individuals but crossing the boundaries of countries.*

3. Samuelson, *op. cit.*, p. 630.
4. *Ibid.*, p. 651.
5. *Ibid.*, p. 628, footnote.
6. *Ibid.*, p. 655.
7. Of course, "productivity" is not inherent in an industry either. As the steel industry and many others illustrate, when an industry is overbuilt, or when it is entered by efficient low-wage workers, its "productivity" declines. This is quite consistent with economic theory. The relevant productivity is *marginal productivity*, which would be reduced by either of these developments. The conventional argument about "the productivity of the American worker" was not good theoretical economics, applying some conception of inherent productivity when the relevant concept was marginal productivity.

8. *Op. cit.*, p. lviii. Tellingly, one sees in the first sentence of the book a clear manifestation of Smith's false conceptualization of inter-

national trade. In the quoted passage, "or in what is purchased with that produce from other nations," Smith presents international trade as (1) *barter exchange* (2) between *nations, as nations*. Implicit in this phrase is the whole fallacy of "the principle of comparative advantage," the automatic balance and the automatic beneficence of international trade. When Smith refers to free trade, the conception that actually is passing through his mind, it seems, is one of barter exchange arranged between nations, not money deals across national boundaries by individuals and firms. This conceptualization, of course, reflects the "classical" idea that what really matter and what define "principles of economics" are *real* or nonmonetary events—which must be hypothetical or imaginary, since actual transactions are monetary ones.

9. As a small but objective indication that even the evidence of recent years has not corrected this deficiency, in a 1984 collection of articles on industrial policy, the word with the longest list of references in the index is none other than "protectionism." Chalmers Johnson, ed., *The Industrial Policy Debate* (San Francisco: Institute for Contemporary Studies, 1984).

10. For a variety of views on this subject, see *ibid.*.

11. That any new fallacies—or new or old truths—on this subject must continue to contend with the ancient fallacies is indicated by this statement: "The arguments for free trade are as true today as they were in the time of Adam Smith. The goal of industrial policy and protectionism is today the same as it was in Smith's time: to subordinate the welfare of the consumer to that of the producer." Bruce Bartlet, "Trade Policy and the Dangers of Protectionism," *ibid.*, p. 169.

12. Robert B. Reich, *The Next American Frontier* (New York: Penguin Books, 1983), p. 127.

13. *Ibid.*, pp. 127–128.

14. Werner L. Chilton, quoted in *The Wall Street Journal*, "Persistent Pay Gap: U. S. Wage Levels Stay Above Foreign Rivals' Despite Restraint Here," April 18, 1984, p. 1.

15. Arthur Neef, quoted in *ibid.*

16. *Ibid.*

17. Paul Hawken, *The Next Economy* (New York: Holt, Rinehart and Winston, 1983), p. 8.

18. On the other hand, basic criticism and rejection of the framework of the orthodox economics has been rising rapidly in recent years. Such criticism goes back to the work of Thornton, Malthus, and Jones in the early 1800s. An alternative and more realistic version of

economics—not based on Natural Harmony—seemed in the early decades of this century to be gaining dominance in the work of American "institutionalist" economists such as Ely, Veblen, and Commons, but recent decades saw a swing back to Smithian economics, now in mathematicized form. Among many recent works that, from one or another viewpoint, make fundamental objections to the orthodox economics are T. W. Hutchison, *Knowledge and Ignorance in Economics* (Chicago: University of Chicago Press, 1977); Kenneth E. Boulding, *Evolutionary Economics* (Beverly Hills: Sage Publications, 1981); Jack Wiseman, ed., *Beyond Positive Economics* (London: The Macmillan Press, 1983); and Lester C. Thurow, *Dangerous Currents: The State of Economics* (New York: Vintage Books, 1984).

Chapter 7 Constructive Policies on International Trade

1. "South Korea Stiffens Countertrade Terms for Foreign Firms Seeking Arms Contracts," and "GATT Countertrade Study," *The Wall Street Journal*, April 17, 1984, p. 37.

2. "South Korea Stiffens Countertrade Terms for Foreign Firms Seeking Arms Contracts," *ibid*.

3. This issue was raised by an official of a United States firm who was interviewed in connection with South Korean countertrade terms: "The great danger for the U. S. is that we're creating our own future competitors. The Koreans want to supply the world." *Ibid*.

Index

Absolute advantage, 99
Adjustment mechanism, and damage to nation, 124–125
 and monetary arrangement, 122–123
Allocation of world resources, international trade and, 175–179
American worker, productivity of, 179–182
Anarchistic kind of freedom, 164
Anarchy, 163, 204
Balance in international trade, implications of, 117–121
Bases of international trade, 54–56
Birth rates, effects of differences in, 149–154
Buy-back arrangement, 220
Capabilities of nations, international trade and, 63–65
Capital, international mobility of, 168–169
Ceteris paribus, misleading use of, 177–178
Challenge of decades ahead, the, 201
Chilton, Werner L., 195
Cipolla, Carlo, 57–58
Colbertism, 166
Colonial nations, and international economic integration, 14, 128–129
Common sense interpretation of recent events, 224
Communications, change in and international economic integration, 13–14
Comparative advantage, 99, 166–172
 as a basic error, 167–168
 doctrine is based on false example, 171
 verbal confusion in, 172
Comparative standards, international trade and, 210–211
Competition, degenerative (*see* Degenerative competition)
 unequal, 103–104
Constructive evolutionary change, 154–156
Contracts, as used by firms and nations, 222–223
Cosmopolitanism, 33–34
Countertrade arrangements, 219–220
Cultural barriers, and international economic integration, 15
Cumulative processes of economic improvement, 66–70
Cybernetics, 12
Darwinian revolution, 9
Decision-levels, 116–117
Degenerative competition, illustrations of, 102–103
 in production standards, 87–92, 213–217

rules to prevent, 102–103
Deindustrialization, 57
Demand, as determining national capabilities, 182–187
"creates its own supply," 184
as explaining United States era of dominance, 185–186
Dependency, international trade and, 93–94
Destructive economic processes, and international trade, 203–204
Discrimination in international trade, 130–132
Disharmony in international trade, 104–105
Diversity and evolutionary change, 208–210
Economic growth, is not equalizing all nations, 205
Economic integration, damage to functional organization of, 41
illustration of effects of, 139–154
Economic strategy, and harmonious-trade area, 110
Economic theory, false interpretation of efficiency of, 45–48
and interpretation of recent events, 224–225
on maximization of world output, 44–45
Economic wants, as in-built, 210
Efficiency, false interpretation of, 45–48, 146–148
and international trade, 173–175
England, economic rise of, 62
Equilibrium income, and international trade, 178–179
Evolutionary processes, 12, 26–27, 145–157, 202–203
constructive, 154–156
and future of mankind, 97
role of population-change in, 149–154
Exchange rates, 123, 143–145
Externalities, defined, 111–112
and harmonious-trade area, 121
importance of, 112–113
and organizational level of decision, 115–116
Fictions, basis of 159
Free trade, as alternative to "protectionism," 187–188
as biased against high-income nations, 164–166
as biased use of language, 11
distinguished from trade between nations, 38–40
as implying the anarchistic kind of freedom, 164
Freedom, conflict among kinds of, 162–164
Gains and losses from international trade, 54–56, 133–134
Government powers, free trade as undermining, 95–97, 204
Group behavior, and societal success, 28–30
Hamilton, Alexander, 103
Harmonious monetary area, 121–125
Harmonious-trade area, defined, 101–105
and discrimination in international trade, 130–132
requirements of, 105–110
whole world as, 110–111
Hawken, Paul, 197
High-income nation, causing survival as, 27–28

Hot-money movements, 93
Ideological barriers to international economic integration, 16–17
Individual rights, and regulation of international dealings, 211–212
Individualism, 31–34
and cosmopolitanism, 33–34
Industrial policy, as cure for West's plight, 189–191
Industries, attractive and unattractive, 120–121
location in various nations of, 135–137
potentially attractive today, 137–138
Insulation of nations, 208–210
International economic integration, barriers to, 13–18
effects of, 18–23
unnatural character of, 22–23
International trade, arranged as trade between nations, 114–117
errors of economic theory on, 44–45
incommensurability of potential gains and losses from, 133–134
as a negative influence, 132–133
significance of, 100
Italian towns, decline of, 57–58
Japan, wage advantage of and industrial policy, 189–190
Jobs, exporting of, 118–119
Knowledge and science, 8–12
Laissez faire doctrine, 160–162
Language abuse, in economics, 160–162

List, Friedrich, 104
Location of industries in different countries, 58–59
effects on capabilities of nations, 63–65
effects of national policies and institutions on, 61–63
Low standard of living, as basis of need for international trade, 55
Low-wage nations, can be damaged by international trade, 49–50
Management of internation trade, 219–221
Markets for advanced goods, and change in living standards, 145–149
which nation gains advantage of, 70–72
Maximization of world output, error of economic theory on, 44–45
Monetary area, harmonious, 121–125
Multi-nation trade arrangements, 222–223
Multinational corporations, and international economic integration, 15–16
Mutualistic dealings, 165
Mutualistic economy, character of, 114–115
and international trade arranged between governments, 39–40
Mutually beneficial international trade, conditions required for, 37–38, 48–49
policy and, 40–41, 203
Mutually rewarding national eco-

nomic exchanges, 24, 125–126
Nation, as essential organizing unit for mankind, 217–218
  as undermined by free trade, 21–22, 41, 95–97, 217–218
  as the unit for economic change, 114, 154–156
National change, as cause-and-effect process, 27–28
National policies and institutions, and international location of industries, 61–63
Nationalization of industry, 220–221
Natural harmony doctrine, 160–162
  contrast of with views of modern science, 31–33
Natural liberty, 160
Natural resources, as basis for international trade, 55–56
Natural rights, and regulation of international trade, 211–212
Nature, as creator of man-serving world, 32–33
Neef, Arthur, 195
New Realist approach to philosophy of science, 11–12
Newton, 9
Oats-and-oranges case, 173–175
Offset arrangements, 219–220
One-world view, 33–34, 208–210
Optimal allocation of resources, international trade and, 175–179
Organizations, separateness required for effectiveness of, 30–31
Overpopulation-caused poverty, international trade and, 42–43, 203–204
Plight of the West, economic theory and, 3–5
  explanations of and remedies for, 188–197, 223–225
Policies toward international trade, kinds of, 127–130
Political disorder, and international economic integration, 14
Poor nations, 206–208
Population, dominating influence of, 81–84
  dynamics of change in, 79–84
  effects of differences in birth rates, 149–154
  and evolutionary path of nation, 81–82
Population explosion, 17, 223
Population-growth, and harmonious-trade area, 107–108
Poverty, spread by international trade, 42–43, 203–204
Poverty-causing factors, that travel only through migration, 72–76
  that travel through international trade, 77–84
Principle of comparative advantage, assumes harmonious-trade area, 111
  as error, 204
Principles, versus cause-and-effect interpretations, 36–37
Production efficiency, and international trade, 173–175
Production standards, and competition-in-third-countries problem, 215–216
  and international-trade policy, 213–217

moral problem in, 216
necessity of differences among nations in, 213–214
unfair competition and, 214
Productivity of the American worker, 179–182
Prosperity, and harmonious monetary area, 121–122
Protectionism, as alternative to free trade, 187–188
Realism, 34–36
  dependence of future of West on, 223–224
  and interpretation of international trade, 50–51
Realist approach to philosophy of science, 11–12
Reich, Robert B., 192–195
Ricardo, David, on principle of comparative advantage, 167–169
Rich nations, 206–208
Rivalrous relations in international trade, 210–211
Routh, Guy, 12
Samuelson, Paul A., 166–167, 170, 175, 176, 179
Second World War, interpretation of economic changes since, 223–224
Selection, 26
Self-evident truths, 9
Separateness, and effectiveness of group or system, 30–31
Side effects of international trade, 53
Small nations, need for international trade of, 54–55
Smith, Adam, as creator of "modern economics," 197
  and factors in international trade, 100
  and neglect of demand in economics, 182–183
  and origin of free-trade doctrine, 166
  on principle of comparative advantage, 167–169
Social behavior, and societal success, 28–30
Social goals, and harmonious-trade area, 108–109
Societal change, as cause-and-effect process, 27–28
Standard of living, effect on market for advanced goods of, 145–149
  potential for cumulative increase in, 66–70
Standards, and harmonious-trade area 108
  kinds of, 89–90
  need of organizations for, 84–85
Standards-lowering competition, 21, 204
  caused by international economic integration, 43–44
  international trade as cause of, 84–92
  prearranged balance in trade and, 120
  ways of dealing with, 213–217
Technically advanced nation, underselling by, 119
Theoretical economics, and modern science, 10
Trade arranged between governments, 219–221
  and logic of mutualistic economy, 39–40
  as only way of assuring mutual

benefit, 40–41
Trade deficit and exchange rate, 143–145
Transportation, changes in and international economic integration, 13–14
Truths, in cause-and-effect world, 159–160
United States, causes of period of economic dominance of, 185–186
Unregulated trade, and "free trade," 38
Wage rates, and balance in international trade, 118–119
effects of decline in, 145–149
equalized by international economic integration, 18–19
and harmonious-trade area, 107
of United States in relation to other countries, 195–196
undercutting of high by low, 142–143, 204–205
Waste, international trade and, 92–93
Wealth of Nations (see Adam Smith)
West, potential futures of 5–8, 134–135

OTHER NEW BOOKS FROM 21ST CENTURY PRESS

Competition, Constructive and Destructive
by John M. Culbertson
about 40 pages, paperback, $2.95
ISBN 0-918357-05-5

In the current debate and controversy over economic regulation and deregulation, proponents of deregulation often assume that "competition" is inherently beneficial. Deregulation, they say, will give us more of this beneficial force, "competition." A contrary view long prominent in economics is that "competition" can be *either constructive or destructive*. It depends on what people or firms *are competing at*. In this view, well designed laws and regulation do not reduce competition. Rather, they *permit constructive competition to prevail*—by preventing the destructive competition that otherwise would displace it.

This booklet will be useful to readers of all kinds who are interested in the hot issue of regulation and deregulation—whether deregulating the banks and the airlines were steps forward, or backward. The booklet also will serve as a supplementary or partial text in economics courses at the introductory and higher levels in microeconomics and industrial organization. The booklet brings in cases that will help students to see the limitations of the theoretical model in which what is needed is only *more* "competition"—which is provided by *laissez faire* policies. It will foster critical thought on the relation of microeconomic theory to realistic analysis of economic policies.

The Dangers of "Free Trade"

by John M. Culbertson
about 40 pages, paperback, $2.95
ISBN 0-918357-03-9

The important ideas presented in *International Trade and the Future of the West* are summarized in this booklet. It will be of interest to readers of all types who are concerned with the future of Western economies and the character of the economic world in which they will be living in the decades ahead. The booklet also will be useful as a supplementary text or partial text in courses in introductory economics, general economics, and international economics. It will provide students with a new view of international trade, and serve as a basis for critical thought and discussion.

Look for these books at your bookstore, or order directly from:

21st Century Press, P. O. Box 5010, Madison, WI 53705.

Send $2.95 plus $.90 for shipping, $3.85, for each booklet. For Wisconsin addresses, add also $.15 sales tax for each booklet.

For quantity use as course textbooks, these booklets are available in text editions at lower cost.